KARGIL

THE INSIDE STORY

In praise of
KARGIL: THE INSIDE STORY

"[Harinder Baweja] exposes some shocking facts about India's lack of battle preparedness. Written as a soldier's diary, *Kargil: The Inside Story* is based on confidential defence documents gleaned from Indian and Pakistani troops in addition to extensive interviews with Indian Army officers and men…

"[She] raises some difficult questions of India's politicians and diplomats, pointing out that they should be concerned that a nuclear powered country is vulnerable to so many operational mistakes… The author does not spare India's scientific establishment either…"

BBC

"A terse, accessible account of one of the darkest episodes in India's history... Written in the form of a soldier's journal, the book grimly recounts the story of the war and the extraordinary courage of the subalterns and officers, while documenting the colossal failure of the top military leadership, its intelligence and of the equipment made available. In short, Baweja is a true professional and this is a professional's book."

India Today

"This is a minor coup where [Baweja's] book scores over others is the peek she's had into confidential military documents and After Action Reports. She recreates with clarity the panic, confusion and initial loss of morale after the deeply unsettling intrusions, inadequate and insufficient maps, ill-prepared troops, unclear orders, and yet the ceaseless demand for quick results that inevitably made soldiers resemble lambs to slaughter. Hard and painful words, these, but familiar for the Indian military now adept at being surprised and back footed by the fog of war."

Hindustan Times

"This book is by the gutsy Harinder Baweja. She saw action on the snowbound mountain peaks on the Indian side of the Line of Control. She has some uncomfortable facts to reveal. Well before our prime minister was embracing his Pakistani counterpart in Lahore, Pakistani Army units were fortifying bunkers on Indian soil. For months our intelligence knew nothing about it. When the action began, our Chief of Staff was in Poland and when it heated up; our General in charge of operations was inaugurating a golf course in Srinagar."

Khushwant Singh
(in his column 'With Malice Towards One and All')

"A very readable and disturbing book. *A Soldier's Diary* provides the insider look at the war. The writer has been long associated with Kashmir and defence-related issues. She provides a unique insight into the war, having been given privileged access to After Action Reports, filed by commanding officers after every action."

Deccan Chronicle

"To give a degree of credibility to her account, Baweja chooses the diary format to present her version of Operation Vijay. The diary reveals how the political leadership and the top brass in the Army had been caught napping and had very little clue about the situation. Days after they sent inadequately armed troops up the barren peaks to push back 'the few rats that have come in.'"

The Hindu

A SOLDIER'S DIARY
KARGIL
THE INSIDE STORY

HARINDER BAWEJA

FOREWORD BY
G.L. BATRA
FATHER OF CAPT VIKRAM BATRA
PARAM VIR CHAKRA

LOTUS COLLECTION
ROLI BOOKS

OTHER LOTUS TITLES

Aitzaz Ahsan	*The Indus Saga: The Making of Pakistan*
Ajay Mansingh	*Firaq Gorakhpuri: The Poet of Pain & Ecstasy*
Amarinder Singh	*The Last Sunset: The Rise & Fall of the Lahore Durbar*
Anil Dharker	*Icons: Men & Women who Shaped Today's India*
Aruna Roy	*The RTI Story: Power to the People*
Bertil Falk	*Feroze: The Forgotten Gandhi*
Dinesh C. Sharma	*Indian Innovation, Not Jugaad: 100 Ideas That Transformed India*
Jenny Housego	*A Woven Life*
Kunal Purandare	*Ramakant Achrekar: A Biography*
Maj. Gen. Ian Cardozo	*Cartoos Saab: A Gorkha Soldier's Story of Bravery and Resolve*
Maj. Gen. Ian Cardozo	*Param Vir: Our Heroes in Battle*
Maj. Gen. Ian Cardozo	*The Sinking of INS Khukri: What Happened in 1971*
Monisha Rajesh	*Around India in 80 Trains*
Murlidhar C. Bhandare	*The Arc of Memory: My Life and Times*
Noorul Hasan	*Meena Kumari: The Poet*
Prateep K. Lahiri	*A Tide in the Affairs of Men: A Public Servant Remembers*
R.V. Smith	*Delhi: Unknown Tales of a City*
Rajika Bhandari	*The Raj on the Move: Story of the Dak Bungalow*
Ralph Russell	*The Famous Ghalib: The Sound of my Moving Pen*
S. Hussain Zaidi	*Dongri to Dubai*
Salman Akthar	*The Book of Emotions*
Shahrayar Khan	*Bhopal Connections: Vignettes of Royal Rule*
Shantanu Guha Ray	*Mahi: The Story of India's Most Successful Captain*
Sharmishta Gooptu	*Bengali Cinema: An Other Nation*
Shrabani Basu	*Spy Princess: The Life of Noor Inayat Khan*
Sobhana K. Nair	*Ram Vilas Paswan: The Weathervane of Indian Politics*
Thomas Weber	*Gandhi at First Sight*
Thomas Weber	*Going Native: Gandhi's Relationship with Western Women*
Vaibhav Purandare	*Sachin Tendulkar: A Definitive Biography*
Vappala Balachandran	*A Life in Shadow: The Secret Story of ACN Nambiar – A Forgotten Anti-Colonial Warrior*
Vir Sanghvi	*Men of Steel: India's Business Leaders in Candid Conversation*

FORTHCOMING TITLE

S. Natesh	*Iconic Trees of India*

To

The infantry soldiers and

my father who served in the

Indian Air Force

Lotus Collection

First published in 2000 by Books Today
This revised edition published in 2018
Third impression, 2024

The Lotus Collection
An imprint of
Roli Books Pvt. Ltd
M-75, Greater Kailash II Market, New Delhi 110 048
Phone: ++91 (011) 4068 2000
info@rolibooks.com
www.rolibooks.com

Also at Chennai, & Mumbai

Cover Design: Bonita Vaz-Shimray
Picture Credits: Getty Images – front cover; insert pages 2-3, 4, 5, 7 (above), 8-9, 12 (above & below); Deepak Das – insert pages 6 (above & below), 7 (below), 10 (above & below), 11
Production: Lavinia Rao
Layout: Bhagirath Kumar

ISBN: 9788193750155

Typeset in Arno Pro by Roli Books Pvt Ltd and
Printed at Saurabh Printers Pvt. Ltd, Delhi.

Contents

Author's Note

Apart from personal, eyewitness accounts, much of the information contained in this book has been obtained from official files which contain the After Action Reports (AAR) filed by units involved in the Kargil conflict. These files are confidential and were shown to the author on the strictest conditions of anonymity. Though disturbing in their content, the real facts regarding India's total lack of preparedness, the cavalier attitude of the top brass in the Indian Army during the crucial initial stages of the conflict and the lack of intelligence, need to be brought out. Not just to ensure that those responsible for such criminal negligence are exposed, but more so, in memory of those courageous men who died defending our borders against impossible, and largely self-imposed, odds.

To protect the identity of the sources, some names have wilfully been changed.

Acknowledgements

For my generation of journalists, Kargil was the first taste of war. Covering it was exciting, full of adventure and very frightening. At all times, the adrenalin kept running. Till the time I finally returned to Delhi and realized I had come back with a lot of emotional baggage. My mind kept travelling back to that evening in July when I stood by the side of a mountain in Drass. Tense soldiers paced up and down, waiting for the stretchers to arrive. Seventeen disfigured bodies were brought down from the heights in two hours.

What was happening in the mountains? What kind of battles did the infantry soldiers have to wage in the deceptively serene snow-capped heights? What went through their minds at 18,000 feet?

We were covering the war from the road heads. Only the officers and jawans could answer the questions. I went back to Kargil in October and spent days and nights talking to them. The answers are as disturbing as the questions. They lived through it; I was only listening to their tales. It was then that I decided to write this book like a soldier would. The book is not a sequence of events nor the last word on the war. It is the story of the infantry battalions who bore the brunt. My deepest gratitude to all those who gave time freely and shared their experiences. I cannot name them but they know who they are.

This book was first published in 2000 by the India Today group, where I then worked. A special thank you to Dilip Bobb, who patiently laboured through my manuscript, and gave it final shape. Many thanks too, to Aroon Purie, for encouraging me to be a danger junkie and to Ashok Chopra, for taking the risk of launching his publishing imprint with my book.

Many thanks to everyone at Roli Books and my friend and publisher Pramod Kapoor for republishing this book and keeping the inside story of Kargil alive.

Finally, my mother, who always encourages, and all my friends, who goad and guide.

Foreword

The Bravery of Capt Vikram Batra, PVC

Col Yogesh Kumar Joshi was ecstatic upon receiving the victory message from Capt Vikram Batra and Capt Sanjeev Jamwal. He started moving towards the peak because, before going for the assault both the young officers had promised to have their morning cup of tea at Point 5140 together. A wave of joy had spread across the brigade and the army headquarters in New Delhi. It was a historical achievement for the Indian Army as well as for India.

The chief of the army, Gen V.P. Malik, personally telephoned Vikram for their battalion's remarkable feat. This was a decisive victory for the 13 Jammu and Kashmir (JAK) Rifles. Col Joshi's eyes were moist as he said, "Not a single soldier died in the operation. The victory of peak 5140 would make a textbook on mountain warfare for the manner in which the operation was carried out. A peak at 17,000 feet was literally snatched from the jaws of a powerful enemy... This is God's grace and the perfect execution of an operation by the youngsters who are the heart, mind and soul of the army."

According to various reports, it was one of India's toughest campaigns in mountain warfare. To reach Point 5140, eight humps had to be crossed. The Pakistanis had deployed machine guns on these peaks and also received artillery support from PoK (Pakistan-occupied Kashmir). However, our valiant fighters achieved the impossible. Photographs of Vikram and his battalion mounting the captured Pakistani gun at the base camp were splashed across the country's newspapers.

Due to his exemplary feat, Vikram was awarded with many titles. He came to be fondly called the 'Tiger of Drass', the 'Lion of Kargil', the 'Kargil Hero', and so on. His bravery, zeal and determination had set a standard for everyone in the troop fighting the battle.

After the victory at Point 5140, an enthusiastic Vikram called us on the morning of June 20, 1999. I received his call and he excitedly said, "Daddy, I have captured my peak." This was his first call after joining the war field.

The satellite phone line was not clear and his words were muffled. He reassured me that he was fine and that he had achieved success in his task. His mother blessed him and encouraged him to continue performing his duty and to never look back. And look back he did not.

Becoming a National Hero

Post the victory at Point 5140, Vikram became a national hero. For four days, he was on TV, recalling his saga of bravery and telling journalists how he led his men to victory. The newspapers carried pictures of weapons seized from the intruders by Vikram and his men.

Vikram became the toast of the media, appearing in a number of interviews. In one of those interviews, he told the reporters that, while capturing Point 5140, they were just 50 metres away from the target, when right in front of them was a patch of snow. The enemy started firing illumination rounds. Vikram and his troops had to lie down there pretending to be dead as the enemy used machine guns and rockets.

Barkha Dutt, a senior journalist covering the Kargil War, interviewed Vikram after the victory over Point 5140. She asked Vikram how he felt after his victory, to which he famously replied, "*Yeh dil maange more,*" which was his victory signal and which he had said to his commanding officer, Col Joshi, after victory over Point 5140 with a big smile. He was brimming with confidence; a pleasant smile on his face and high energy levels indicated a sense of pride.

With the capture of Point 5140, the course of battle was turned towards further victories, and the morale of our army was boosted. Vikram's name was also recommended for the Maha Vir Chakra award, the second-highest military decoration of the country. But he had no full stop here.

Bravery at Point 4875

After the capture of Point 5140, the troops (led by Vikram and Capt Jamwal) had to station there for a few days, as there were chances of a counter-attack by the enemy. They stayed at the top till June 26 to strengthen the defence and reshape the bunkers, and then returned to the base camp to rest and re-energize for a few days. They could not rest for more than three to four days, as the condition on other peaks was worsening.

While trying to capture Point 4875, Indian troops were pinned down by heavy firing from the other side. Point 4875 had to be reinforced, and Col Joshi had to decide who would head the mission. Fresh from his victory, Vikram again volunteered to lead the troops. Using tired troops in operations again and again is dangerous, but when the operations are continuous, there is no alternative.

Such was the zeal and enthusiasm of the soldiers that despite the strict rules that dictate that soldiers cannot question the orders of their seniors, several soldiers pleaded for permission to accompany Vikram even at the cost of earning the severe displeasure of their commanding officers. They were so enthused with Vikram's voluntary act that they were willing to be court-martialled for the sake of accompanying him.

Point 4875 was an extremely difficult mission. This peak was heavily impounded by the enemy, and the Pakistani artillery had its guns targeted at the whole stretch of about 30–40 kilometers of National Highway 1A from Drass to Matayen. Any vehicle passing through this route could be easily targeted and destroyed. Even helicopter landing had become impossible.

The Final Battle

"I will either come back after raising the Indian flag in victory or return wrapped in it."

It is hard to imagine the extreme conditions prevailing on heights such as Point 4875. This was one of the most crucial peaks. Regaining it would strengthen India's hold on the Valley.

Over the next few days, after coming back home from college, I would watch the evening news on TV to get any updates on my son. I recall that a TV correspondent had managed to reach the base camp and interview Vikram, asking him to share his feelings. Vikram replied, "Our government is taking care of the supply of our food material and other things to the best of its abilities at such high altitude. It is a tough task. I also wish that the families of the deceased soldiers are looked after well by the government and society." His commanders appreciated his mature reply (he was all of 24 years old then, and the youngest captain on the Kargil battlefield), but hundreds of miles away, at home, when I saw Vikram on television, my heart sank. I could read the expression on his face. After speaking to the reporter, he just turned his face away from the camera. I turned away from the television screen and broke down as I doubted his safe return back home. I remember my wife asking me why I had gone so silent suddenly; I could not tell her what I felt.

At 1 p.m. on July 5, our troops captured Point 4875. But the enemy continued to fire from a position north of the point. It became evident that this post had to be conquered. A strong contingent of enemy troops could be seen on a long and narrow ledge running north of Point 4875. To secure our position, it was necessary to clear the ledge. The battle continued the entire day. On July 6, it was reported that our troops could not sustain firefighting of such intensity without reinforcements. The reinforcements were immediately brought up. A fresh wave of enthusiasm coursed through the exhausted troops. Through interception of the radio frequencies, the enemy got wind of Vikram's presence. Once again they threatened him on his radio: "*Sher Shah, upar toh aa gaye ho, lekin wapis nahi jane denge; Inshallah, upar hi bhej denge.*" (Sher Shah, you have come this far, but you will not go back alive. Inshallah, we'll kill you.) An undaunted Vikram replied, "*Upar toh tumhe aur tumhare sathion ko jana hoga.*" (It is you and your companions who will be killed.)

On July 6–7, Vikram volunteered to head a party and reach this ledge even though he was unwell. Due to high fever and fatigue, his eyes were red as he sat wrapped in a blanket. Looking at Vikram's condition, his commanding officer hesitated to send him to the battlefront, but Vikram insisted. Motivated by Vikram's offer, many soldiers volunteered to accompany him. Vikram and the soldiers began their arduous trek. From eyewitnesses, I heard later that, while still at the task, somewhere along the climb, suddenly Vikram's face changed. The signs of fatigue and fever vanished. He became a man fired by a mission.

The chilling winds of Mushkoh Valley penetrated the bones of our soldiers. It was pitch-dark. The climb was almost vertical. To make matters worse, it began to snow. Vikram continued to move like a snow leopard. He coaxed and encouraged his exhausted troops to press on. Then he heard the rat-a-tat of a machine gun, which had pinned down his troops. Vikram swiftly moved towards the firing gun by hiding behind a rock and then ran to the shelter of the next, till he reached close to the gun, lobbed a hand grenade, and destroyed it. He then asked his troops to follow him. They advanced to the next position since the enemy guns had to be silenced before daylight.

Vikram moved ahead, firing constantly with his AK-47. Fearlessly, he closed in on the enemy. It was a fight at such close quarters that he could no longer use his rifle. He pulled out his bayonet and charged at the enemy. He grappled with a Pakistani soldier, floored him with a punch on the nose, and plunged his bayonet into him. Another intruder attacked him from behind. Vikram threw him off his back and pierced him with his bayonet. A machine gun was firing from the ledge. Vikram jumped inside the ledge, where two soldiers were feeding the gun and another was firing it. A junior officer of the Pakistani Army was supervising them. Vikram leaped inside and single-handedly killed all five of them. However, he was outnumbered and was shot at close range.

Vikram, with another young officer, Anuj Nayyar, fought off the enemy's counter-attack ferociously. They cleared all the enemy bunkers, encouraged their men to go forward, engaged in hand-to-hand combat, and forced the Pakistanis to retreat.

On July 7, the mission was almost over, when Vikram ran out of his bunker to rescue another officer, Lt Naveen Anaberu, whose legs had been severely injured in an explosion. The subedar of his battalion begged him not to leave and offered to go instead. But Vikram famously told him, "*Tu baal-bachchedar hai, hat ja peeche.*" (You have a wife and children, step aside.) He lunged forward to save the young Lt Naveen Anaberu. As Vikram was dragging Naveen towards cover, the gravely wounded officer pleaded with Vikram to let him continue the fight. Just then a bullet pierced through Vikram's chest. Vikram was martyred, but he managed to save the life of Lt Naveen.

Enraged by Vikram's death, the soldiers of the 13 JAK Rifles pursued the enemy. A soldier from the battalion told Gaurav Sawant, a TV correspondent, "Nobody was bothered about the bullets flying in any direction. There was only one thing on everybody's mind: to avenge Capt Batra's death." Those who survived later reported that Vikram died with the words '*Jai Mata Di*' (Victory to Mother Durga) on his lips.

Unnerved by the fury of the attack, the Pakistanis fell back. The Indian soldiers gained the upper hand. Captain Batra's sacrifice paved the way for the success of our troops and the consolidation of the Indian hold on Point 4875.

Sawant, in his book *Dateline Kargil* writes, "Vikram Batra had succeeded in clearing the ledge, securing the peak and also the movement of the 17 Jat troops pinned down by effective Pakistani firing under the guidance of Col Dinesh Badola."

Another TV journalist, Srinjoy Chowdhury, covering the war, writes in his book *Despatches from Kargil*, "Vikram would volunteer for the most difficult tasks, climbing up a sheer rock face to take the enemy in the rear. And how thin the margins between death and glory are! This time there was no return to adulation, no TV cameras, just a few tears and a letter home. A hidden machine-gun opened up; he crawled up and silenced it with a volley of grenades. When three enemy soldiers rushed out, he killed them all, but was seriously wounded in the firefight. He refused to be evacuated; he would regroup his men and charge towards the final defences, dying in the effort. They didn't give him the Param Vir Chakra for nothing."

By the morning of July 8, India had won Point 4875 but lost Capt Vikram Batra. With the conquest of Point 4875, the connectivity to Ladakh was secured and our vehicles could move freely on the Srinagar–Leh Highway.

The day his body was brought home, it was excruciating. With tears coursing down her cheeks, my wife said, "No parent can see the dead body of their young son. Our son had captured three peaks, he had taken the nation by storm, but suddenly he was no more. Yet, when God gives you a mortal blow, he gives you the strength to cope with the grief. Guru Gobind Singh sacrificed four sons for the country. Maybe there was some reason that God gave me twins – one had been marked for the country and one for me."

When one of Vikram's friends had told him to be careful since war had begun, he had replied, "Don't worry. I will either come back after raising the Indian flag in victory or return wrapped in it." Vikram fulfilled both his assertions. He raised India's victorious tricolour at the height of 17,000 feet when he captured Point 5140. Later, when he fell fighting at Point 4875, his body was brought back home wrapped in our national flag. Such was the bravery and patriotism of our son Vikram.

Point 4875 has been renamed 'Captain Batra Top', and the transit camp in Drass where weary soldiers break their journey has come to be known as Capt Batra Transit Camp. Capt Anuj

Nayyar was awarded the Maha Vir Chakra, the second-highest military decoration for bravery. For his sustained display of conspicuous leadership of the highest order in the face of adversity, Vikram was posthumously awarded India's highest military decoration, the Param Vir Chakra.

Memoir of our First Visit to Drass (Kargil)

It was in July 2002, the Kargil Vijay Diwas, that we were called by Vikram to those insurmountable heights of Drass and Kargil. We set out for our journey via Srinagar, where we were received by the army authorities and were given full cover. The feeling of pride, as if we were visiting our beloved son as a commanding officer, was spiraling through our veins.

The treacherous journey to Drass, wherein we crossed the Zoji La pass (the second-highest motorable pass in the world) was breathtaking. On one side were icy glaciers and on the other, a deep valley – the like of which one could have imagined only in dreams. The liaison officer accompanying us recounted all the details of the war the Indian Army had fought and mentioned Vikram's bravery. We felt as if we were travelling with Vikram, understanding the army tactics and the way the men in uniform dared to challenge the enemy that had infiltrated our terrain.

We were received warmly by one of the colonels and stayed at Capt Vikram Batra (PVC) Transit Camp. It had small huts, and each one was named after the gigantic peaks our army had captured (Batra Top, Tololing, Tiger Hill, etc.). The mixed bag of emotions running through the heart and mind were making us both beam with pride and reverence, but it also had the pinch of having lost our brave son at such a young age.

Looking at Tiger Hill from the transit camp was a sight that still runs through our memories. A hundred meters on the left was Point 4875 (now called Batra Top). The image left us wondering at the grit Vikram had shown. It was as if he was still commanding those peaks and safeguarding the Indian border.

After the sunset we were invited to dine with Corps Commander Lt Gen Katoch. It was as if Vikram were hosting his parents for the lovely dinner at the ground base of Drass Town, talking about the bravery he and his fellow soldiers had displayed while capturing Point 5140 and Point 4875.

The bigger surprise came when the sepoy who had carried the food and other weapons on the pony when Vikram was leading the assault during his last mission met us. He recounted Vikram's virtues and heroism in detail. We were still wondering how, while it had been three years since he had laid down his life, he still commanded those icy peaks. We were told that we could visit Point 4875, which was 17,500 feet above sea level, but our age and health did not permit us. We tried to see those peaks through a telescope.

The journey would not have been complete without touching the soil where Vikram laid down his life. It was an overwhelming gesture when the corps commander gifted us with two glasses filled with the soil of Point 4875 and Tololing. For us, it was nothing less than visiting a pilgrimage site. Though our eyes were moist and our feelings strong, we were proud of the legacy Vikram left behind, etching a name for himself in the annals of Indian history. We felt his spiritual presence in the environment of Drass.

Our Thoughts after Vikram's Martyrdom

We had never imagined that a son could make his parents worthy of the amount of honour we received from people across our country after his martyrdom. He has elevated our status to that of proud parents of a Param Vir Chakra recipient.

I was overwhelmed with the honour that I received at Surat (Gujarat) when I passed through the roads, stretching about 20 kilometres, on a chariot. I was wearing a turban and heavy floral garlands. There were two more chariots occupied by two other surviving PVCs. About four lakh citizens of Surat were standing on both sides of the road and showering flower petals on us. It raised my emotions. With tears in my eyes I thought of him, and wished my son could have received this honour in his own life.

In August 2010, my wife and I were travelling from Delhi to Nagpur by an Indigo Airlines flight. Our seats were far back, numbering 25 and 26. We were pleasantly taken aback when one of the crew members asked us to move to seats in front and offered us a platter of eatables as a token of gratitude. To our utter surprise the crew then announced that the parents of Late Capt Vikram Batra, PVC were with them on the flight. The passengers were requested to accord their regards by standing and applauding for us. We noticed that all the eyes were looking for us. We kept sitting so that they could identify us and then we also stood up to reciprocate their feelings. At the Nagpur airport, it was heartening to see all the crew members standing at the exit point and presented us a bouquet and a framed photograph of Vikram with insignia of the airlines on the background. We were certainly overwhelmed by the recognition and the honour given to the martyrdom of our son.

Capt Naveen Anaberu once shared with me how he met Vikram on his first day at IMA Dehradun. Being late at the mess for dinner, he was told that the food was almost over. There was just one cadet still eating his dinner. Naveen sat along with him to get acquainted. Within a few minutes the young cadet pushed his plate towards Naveen and said that they could share the food.

He was none other than Vikram and soon they became friends. Naveen said, "Being senior to me, he used to tell me about the army ethics and war strategies. It was completely unpredictable that I would fight the war under his command during Kargil war and he would be my saviour. What a coincidence that the same Vikram became my commander of the Delta Company of 13 JAK Rifles, and rescued me without caring for his life when I got hit by a hand grenade. He came as a divine force to save my life. When I was shrieking with extreme pain, he jumped out of the bunker and within no time, carried me to a safe place and continued the fight at my post."

Brig MPS Bajwa, Commander of 192 Brigade during the Kargil war, reserved special praise for Vikram. Vikram's unit was under his brigade while they were operating in Sopore from 1997 to early '99. He had met Vikram after one of the encounters in Sopore and told him to do well in his future operations. Vikram assured him that he would not let any enemy or militant escape. Incidentally, after the battle of Point 5140, Vikram happened to meet Brig Bajwa at the brigade headquarters. He said, "Sir as I had promised, I cleared all the enemy posts at the top." Brig Bajwa beamed with pride and patted his back. Sadly, we lost Vikram a few days later.

Many years later, Brig Bajwa, on national television said, "*Vikram ko do Paramvir Chakra dete toh bhi kam tha.*" (Even if Vikram was given two PVCs it was less.) That is a huge compliment from someone so senior. It fills my heart with pride.

Though we miss him every moment, we feel that he is always with us spiritually. The departure of a noble son is of course painful, but to bring forth such a son is also great luck. We will always be proud of him.

G.L. Batra

Father of Capt Vikram Batra

Introduction

In the jagged heights of Kargil, the signs of battle have long been obliterated. It is twenty-five long years since the mountains reverberated with the constant sound of artillery fire. India fought a sharp though short war in a rugged, remote and inhospitable corner that few had even heard of. Kargil, Drass, Mushkoh, Batalik were mere names till the media brought them into ordinary drawing rooms.

Even the names of locations in the war theatre bear testimony to just how desolate and isolated this part of India is: Point 4875, Point 5140, Point 4812. They were just geographical references, restricted to strategic maps in the offices of army commanders, until Kargil exploded into life, in full colour, on television screens.

India emerged victorious in July 1999, but paid a heavy price. The Indian Army and the Air Force lost over 500 men. As many as 1,109 were wounded. Several post-mortems were done after Nawaz Sharif, the then prime minister of Pakistan was ordered by the president of the United States of America to withdraw his troops from Indian territory. Within 72 hours of the army declaring victory on July 26, 1999 – referred to as

Vijay Diwas – the government set up its first committee, under the chairmanship of K. Subrahmanyam, to "review the events leading up to the Pakistani aggression in the Kargil District of Ladakh in Jammu & Kashmir," and recommend measures, "considered necessary to safeguard national security against such armed intrusions."

The committee was scathing in its report. "The Review Committee had before it overwhelming evidence that the Pakistani armed intrusion in the Kargil sector came as a complete and total surprise to the Indian government, army and intelligence agencies as well as to the J&K state government and its agencies. The Committee did not come across any agency or individual who was able clearly to assess before the event, the possibility of a largescale Pakistani military intrusion across the Kargil heights," it said at the outset. No intelligence agency had any inkling of the fact that Pakistan was putting an audacious plan into action, in the peak of winter, braving avalanches and blizzards.

The committee made several recommendations, many of which have been implemented, including better coordination between the various intelligence agencies. Two sentences from the committee's report, stand out, a quarter century after the guns have fallen silent over the frigid wasteland in Kargil. They, in fact, are key to the oft-asked question of whether Kargil can be repeated. "Pakistan's action at Kargil was not rational. Its behaviour patterns require to be carefully studied in order to gain a better understanding of the psyche of its leadership," the report observed.

Does India's security establishment have a better understanding of Pakistan's 'psyche'? Has India learnt its lessons from Kargil? The continuing assaults on India –

over the two and a half decades since Kargil – provide some answers.

India has been hit multiple times. In less than two years after the Kargil conflict, Pakistani-trained terrorists attacked the Indian Parliament in December 2001. The assault on the temple of India's democracy brought India and Pakistan to the brink of war once again and the armies of the two nations were caught in an eyeball-to-eyeball confrontation for several months.

Despite a complete analysis of the need to shore-up the country's intelligence-gathering abilities, ten armed terrorists sailed to Mumbai, all the way from Karachi and held the financial nerve-centre hostage for over 72 hours, killing 166 innocents. The gaps in India's security establishment were prised open once again and several post-mortems done. Several prime ministers, I.K. Gujral, Manmohan Singh, and the more muscular-oriented Narendra Modi have been tested by Pakistan and its proxies.

Modi took the risk of allowing an ISI representative to be part of a Joint Investigations Team that visited India after another audacious attack on an air force base in Pathankot, but Pakistan has done little – if nothing – to bring the terrorists to book. After the Pathankot attack, the advisor to the Pakistani prime minister admitted to the fact that the terrorists had made telephone calls to the Jaish-e-Mohammad headquarter in Bahawalpur but the investigation made no headway.

Pakistan continues to hit India through non-state actors. The suicide attack on an army camp in Kashmir's Uri in August 2016 forced Modi to take political ownership of the surgical strikes that followed, but the strikes have failed to deter Pakistan.

The assaults have also exposed the chinks in India's armour. Fidayeens, determined to destroy and die, have repeatedly managed to find their way into well-guarded installations. They did that in Pathankot, where they even spent a night, undetected. Suicide squads managed to cut the wire and kill 18 unsuspecting soldiers in Uri. In January 2018, another squad breached the security to enter an army installation in Jammu's Sunjuwan.

In another brutal assault in February 2019 – months before the general election – a suicide bomber killed 40 CRPF troopers. A local Kashmiri belonging to the Jaish-e-Mohammad rammed an explosive-laden car into the CRPF convoy in South Kashmir's Pulwama.

Modi, who had redrawn the security matrix after Uri, used the Indian Air Force to carry out punitive strikes at a Jaish facility in Pakistan's Balakot. The Modi government has sent out clear signals of a zero tolerance policy and refuses to engage with Pakistan. Talks and terrorism cannot go hand in hand, he and his ministers have reiterated.

He and his government have now taken on a more belligerent tone and the new mantra is, *"ghar mein ghus ke mare gein"* (We will enter your house and kill you).

In 1999, Pakistan had entered our 'ghar' in the hope of internationalising the Kashmir issue. There have been no major terror strikes after Pulwama but the contours of terrorism have changed. Pakistan is still sending in mercenaries and the terror infrastructure is intact.

India cannot afford to lower its guard. It is now also facing a challenge on its border with China. The question then is, what is the level of India's preparedness?

In a signed column, written sixteen years after Kargil, General V.P. Malik – who was the chief of army staff during the war – said, "Our western border is much better manned than before. More troops have been deployed on the LoC and a border fence has been constructed. We also have surveillance satellites, unmanned aerial vehicles, thermal imagers, radars and ground sensors, which were non-existent in 1999. But apart from that, we do not seem to have learnt any important lessons from that war. The modernisation of the armed forces continues to lag behind. The existing state of weapons and equipment could be sufficient for border skirmishes, but if they escalate, which can never be ruled out, deficiencies of weapons and ammunition and the lack of modernisation will make the present day Chiefs repeat what I had said long ago – 'We shall fight with whatever we have.' Over the years, our capability to deter the adversary has been seriously eroded."

The vulnerability is more than evident. His words remind me of what I witnessed for the two months that I was in Kargil.

In 1999, young officers and men won the day for the nation, despite unimaginable odds: shortage of men and machines, guns that didn't open up, missile warheads that didn't fire.

Twenty-five years after Kargil, the question of, have we learnt our lessons, still remains relevant. General Malik provided some answers but here is what a 2017 report by the Comptroller and Auditor General of India (CAG) found: 61 of 152 types of ammunition, considered critical by the Indian Army to fight a war, were available for just ten days. The report, tabled in Parliament in July pointed out that the army is meant to hold ammunition to fight a twenty-day war.

Ironically, that is the last report on the preparedness of the armed forces in the public domain. CAG is still doing its audits and submitting their reports to Parliament but not uploading them on its site. The only clue to India's current preparedness is contained in a statement put out by the audit agency in 2023. It said, "The Comptroller and Auditor General of India has flagged that the replacement of existing artillery guns with state-of-the-art guns has been progressing at a 'slow pace' for over last two decades."

The reason why the reports are not being made available were revealed by Rajiv Mehrishi, the head of the audit institution, who retired in 2020. He said it was his decision to not upload reports relating to defence audits.

He detailed how the 2017 report regarding the lack of ammunition caused a controversy. Posted in the home ministry then, Mehrishi in an interview later to the *Indian Express* said, "When I was in Home [Ministry], there was a lot of tension with Pakistan. At that time, there was a CAG report detailing a shortage of ammunition. Basically, if there is a shortage, then at least the enemy should not know about it… At least we are not making it available on the tap of a button. *Koi Washington me dekh raha hai, Beijing me bhi dekh raha hai, Islamabad mein bhi dekh raha hai.* (The report was being seen in Washington, Beijing and Islamabad.) Therefore, we took a decision."

For the sake of transparency – vital in any democracy – it is imperative that the true story of Kargil not become a mere footnote in history. The true story of what transpired in Kargil needs to be revealed.

The country saw politicians saluting bodies of soldiers laid out in coffins. They did not see the blood that was spilt, the young men who died such horrible deaths so that all of us could sleep easier at night. These scenes were not shown live on television. These were scenes I saw, and will never forget. Bravery and supreme sacrifice are mere words, phrases written on commendations and citations at medal ceremonies. Yet, for those of us who were there, and saw the shattered limbs and the bloody remains, and heard the screams of agony and the unending, nerve-numbing explosions of artillery, it was a humbling lesson in what courage and heroism is really about. It is also a reminder of what makes Kashmir such a volatile, emotive issue.

This book, however, is not my story. Many of my media colleagues, who were with me on those unforgiving heights, have penned their accounts. For my part, I can do no less in honour of those courageous warriors, than reproduce a soldier's diary of one of the many faceless men who fought for honour, his unit, for country and family, and lived to tell his tale. It moved me in immeasurable ways.

For most part, the book is drawn from the army's own reports. I can only hope it serves as a reminder of what our soldiers suffered, and endured.

ONE

"Some rats have come in"

MAY 13

The scene that greets us is chaotic. This is the Traffic Check Post (TCP) at Sonamarg. Ahead, the road twists and turns, leading to Kargil. Both sides of the road are choked with endless convoys of army vehicles. Like us, all the units that have been rushed here have done so virtually overnight. Most have been hastily pulled out from CI Ops, army shorthand for Counter-Insurgency Operations, in the Kashmir Valley. Some, like 1 Naga, were awaiting transfer orders after a gruelling stint in Siachen. Most of their men were on leave. They have arrived here at just about half strength. We are all here because of a typical army-style briefing. In tones terse and cryptic, we were told: "Some rats have come in."

Translated, it meant that there had been some incursion into Indian territory by Pakistan-backed militants. This, however, was clearly no routine crossover. The large number of vehicles and the number of units that had been rushed here – 8 Sikh, 1 Naga, 12 Jammu & Kashmir Light Infantry, and 18 and 16 Grenadiers, which was the holding unit for the Drass–Kargil sector – clearly implied that this was more serious than usual. Yet, in all our briefings so far, the attitude of senior army commanders had been exactly the opposite. Back in the Valley, a Major-General, the man in charge of CI Ops in the area, repeated in his briefing that we were being sent to Kargil to evict 'some Paki rats', the phrase underlining the assessment by Army Headquarters in South Block and Srinagar, that we were dealing with a minor intrusion. In fact, so lightly was the threat treated that officers and men of 16 Grenadiers still had their families with them. Even in our unit, most of us had written or sent messages to friends and relatives saying we would be back soon.

The sense of unease among the officers huddled by the side of the road at the TCP was growing by the hour. What was going on? Why were we being told nothing? Where were the intelligence inputs? Where was the detailed briefing on enemy strength, positions and fortifications? There were other questions that needed answering. Why the unusual point of ingress? Why through Kargil? Why through a Shia-dominated area where shelter is difficult? Here, the local population is not sympathetic to the so-called independence movement. They have lived in near-total isolation from the Kashmir Valley where shutters are hastily downed a little before sunset. Kargil and Drass are, figuratively, a million miles from the slogans and chants of *hum kya chahte, azadi* (we want independence). Far from the scenes of violence and the omnipresent gun barrels and sandbags. Why, then, had the infiltrators chosen these desolate mountains? It was a question to which our field commanders had no initial answer. In fact, the real answer was to become, for an excessive number of brave soldiers, their epitaph.

Our convoy snaked its way past the bends, the three tonners groaning as they crawled up the narrow Zoji La pass at 11,600 feet. For the superstitious, the date had an ominous ring. As our convoy moved past the TCP and along the road that represents Kargil's lifeline, there was an even more ominous warning. The driver of my vehicle suddenly braked. Our convoy had been waved down by a colonel camped alongside the road. He thrust his head into the commanding officer's or CO's vehicle and shouted hysterically, "Don't go ahead, you will all be killed. They are dominating the road... you will all be butchered." The Colonel, an artillery officer, had already had a taste of the enemy firepower. He had been under an incessant rain of shells fired from across the border and from the heights now occupied by the 'rats'.

We were given our share soon enough, our vehicles shaken by huge explosions which carved out chunks of the mountain. There was dust everywhere, barely settling before another shell sailed in, and another and another. The terrain was already pockmarked with craters. The earth shook. Through the haze, I could still hear the colonel's voice repeating, "Don't move forward. Believe me, you will all be butchered. Soon it will be dark and you cannot drive with your headlights on. That's an invitation to death." We asked the Colonel where we could find the brigade commander, Brigadier Surinder Singh, the officer in-charge of the Kargil sector. He gave us directions and we found the Brigadier sitting in a bunker in a tracksuit, a blanket thrown around his legs. We reported the arrival of our unit and Surinder Singh, as always wearing a ready smile, said, "Don't worry, some *atankwadis* (militants) have come in. We will catch them by the scruff of their necks and throw them out."

"We don't know the terrain, sir," our CO replied.

"Don't worry, the commanding officer of 16 Grenadiers will brief you. I will give you a task tomorrow morning," he said, bidding us good night.

We stayed on the roadside that night, most of the unit huddled in their vehicles. Sleep was impossible amidst the thunder of artillery fire and the roar of guns. It was a foretaste of what we were headed into, a deadly killing zone where the enemy was not just artillery shells and fanatical soldiers, but the weather and terrain as well.

All of us officers and company commanders feel a sharpened sense of responsibility. We are leading men who will follow us to hell, bound by tradition and faith, unquestioning, ever-obedient, unmindful of the danger or threat to their own lives. I am filled with a sense of dread.

MAY 14

We conducted a quick survey of the arms and ammunition we were carrying. The unit we had relieved had handed over their weapons to us in a crisis situation, the handover lasting till 3 a.m. It was the only way we could have moved, as we had been ordered to, by May 13. Like many other units which converged hurriedly on Kargil, we were woefully short of weaponry. We don't have enough rocket launchers and only one of the five radio sets is functional. Automatic Grenade Launchers, Machine Guns, Faggot missiles. They are all listed but the numbers under the column "Deficit" far outweighs the column for "Authorization". Batteries... we are even short of batteries. We are also short on news about the intrusions, the enemy force, their strength or their defences. "There is some problem in Kargil" is all that 15 Corps, the Srinagar-based operational headquarters, told us. The official word, even two days after our arrival, was that "some militants have crossed over".

Finally, news has started trickling in. The "infiltrators" had first been noticed on May 5. Three days later, when a patrol was sent to investigate, they returned with four of their men in body bags.

A clearer picture emerged after I met officers from 1 Naga, the infantry unit which was among the first to move into Drass. Their experience was to prove a dangerous portent of what was to follow over the next few days: the army brass and the Defence Ministry playing down the threat while soldiers continued to die under circumstances which should never have been allowed to happen. What this resulted in was total and suicidal confusion. The commanding officer of 1 Naga had this to say in his After Action Report (in which the unit outlines its tasks and experiences during the battle, spells out the lessons learnt and makes recommendations): "On May 12, the unit had not even started acclimatizing when it was asked to deploy one company in small groups in Tololing nallah and Bimbac nallah. The rest were asked to be ready to move at short notice. The same day again, orders were received for one company to move to Mushkoh Valley in 4754 and occupy defences. In the evening, further orders were received from 121 Brigade Headquarters (commanded by Brigadier Surinder Singh) to move one company to Kargil, which also left immediately. One remaining company was asked to move and be deployed on the southern spur of Point 4590. On May 13, at 2000 hours, orders were received to again concentrate all companies at Drass including the company which had moved to Kargil. By first light on May 14, the officiating commander was briefed by Commander, 121 on the impending task of the unit..."

It was clear from this that confusion prevailed. His report raised some serious questions. Where was the command and control? How many infiltrators were there? More importantly, where were they? How many troops were needed to tackle them, and where? 121 Brigade certainly didn't know. Neither did 15 Corps. Nor did Northern Command at Udhampur, or the Army Headquarters in Delhi. In fact, in a bizarre sequence of events, the army chief, General Ved Prakash Malik, was away in Poland the day our unit arrived in Drass. The very fact that he was out of the country and in no hurry to rush back only added to the dangerous sense of complacency at the top.

15 Corps was the hub, the operational headquarters overseeing the war theatre. It got its inputs from 121 Brigade and disseminated information up the line to Northern Command at Udhampur and Army Headquarters in Delhi. But it also had its own independent sources of information. What was its intelligence wing doing? Were they as much in the dark as everybody else?

The entire chain of command seemed to be in the dark. It was the only explanation for their indecisiveness. Why send one company to Mushkoh and dispatch another to Kargil and then get them all back again between 2000 hours on May 13 and first light, May 14? Driving the 60 km stretch from Drass to Kargil was not without peril.

The artillery shells meant driving through a hail of steel. One officer returned from the 15 Corps Headquarters at Srinagar and the briefing he had had from the corps commander, Lt Gen Krishan Pal and his team was not very different. "Some people have come in. It is a localized affair. Take them on and throw them out," were the orders he had been given. For a long time after our arrival, we continued to address the enemy as 'they'. In briefings, we were continuously told 'they' were 'militants' and 'mercenaries'.

It is the kind of situation that is every soldier's nightmare. To go into battle with a total lack of information, under a confused leadership, conflicting orders, no intelligence about the enemy force, their motivation, their numbers, their defences; their weaponry. Or even their identity: were they regular soldiers or mujahideen?

MAY 15

That impression was reinforced the next day. Here are the operational orders given to 1 Naga by Commander, 121 Brigade, on this day:

(a) One company to move through Bimbat nallah to attack Point 5140 (Tololing Top) from Northern direction and capture the objective by first light, 17 May;

(b) Three companies to move along axis Drass-Sando-Point 5100 via Gorkha nallah and capture Point 5100, hold feature with one platoon and move along ridgelines to secure area Point 4700. Thereafter to marry up with the company at Point 5140 and capture area Hump and Point 4590 with one company.

There are approximately 15 to 16 militants who were scattered in the area as follows:

(a) Enemy observation post at Point 5100 with 3 to 4 militants;

(b) Suspected militants located at Point 4700;
(c) 4 to 5 militants at Point 5140;
(d) 6 to 8 militants at Point 4590.

Fifteen to sixteen militants! What are a handful of militants in the face of an entire infantry battalion? Moreover, that still didn't explain the amount of artillery the Pakistan Army was raining down on the area. Even as covering fire for militant infiltration, this was highly excessive. The sound and fury of artillery shells was unceasing. By now, our own artillery units had moved their field guns into position to retaliate. Both sides were firing at each other across mountains that stood at 15,000 to 20,000 feet. The noise and destruction were awesome. Yet, our commanders in the field kept insisting it was a minor intrusion and the 'rats' would be thrown out soon. The bedlam was confounded when operational plans were hurriedly made. There were no estimates of enemy strength for each feature, no guides, not even terrain maps.

We were luckier than the officers and men of 1 Naga. They had been inducted from CI Ops at short notice and a large part of the battalion was on leave due to its impending move to Siachen. They were ordered to move to Drass almost overnight, so the effective strength of each company was only 50 to 55 men. If that was not bad enough, the unit was rushed into an operation within hours of their arrival, without a single day of acclimatization, without time to get used to the rarefied atmosphere and, above all, not equipped for high altitude warfare. They had no snowshoes, no special clothing required for heights above 12,000 feet. Nor did they have local guides. All they were told was: You have to capture the objective by first light. Even the maps they were given were photocopies.

There is more to this tragic tale of confusion and neglect. They did not have a single Medium Machine Gun and were issued INSAS rifles, a weapon they were totally unfamiliar with. For counter-insurgency operations, they used AK-47s. The officers and men of 1 Naga had never trained with these rifles. They didn't even know its range. In the confusion, such minor matters were brushed aside. How many lives could have been saved? And how many were lost? History will never be able to judge. In the eventual afterglow of victory, those responsible for such crass negligence will not be touched. Instead, they will probably be promoted.

MAY 16

Back at Drass, we were faced with the realization that we were not any better off than the men of 1 Naga. When the sun was slowly setting, the last rays briefly lighting up the shadows settling in on the snow-capped peaks, we received an urgent call from Brigade Headquarters. "Be prepared to launch a company for emergency operations. Send the company commander for a briefing," was the terse message. The Battalion's 2iC (second in command), Major Arun Suri, was asked to prepare for the task. Arun wasn't even supposed to be in Drass. He had been posted to another unit while we were still in the Valley, but was reverted back after the battalion was asked to proceed to the battleground. Covering a distance of barely eight kilometres, from where our unit had pitched tents to the makeshift Brigade headquarters in Pandrass, was a nerve-wracking experience. Driving through the darkness that had now enveloped the area, the silence of the still night being broken by sharp, staccato sounds of shells arching overhead, Arun reached Brigade Headquarters.

Brigadier Surinder Singh was no longer smiling. He was in a sombre mood. His instructions to Arun were to divide the company into section groups and place them around Tiger Hill. The various points the men were to occupy were chalked out on a map laid out on a rickety table. While Arun was away getting briefed, our CO's radio set buzzed. It was Brigadier Surinder Singh complaining about Arun. "This officer is arguing too much!" screamed the Brigade Commander, "This is the task that has been assigned and I want it done..." A little later, a visibly angry Arun strode into the tents where we were seated. "They have no information," he burst out, "They can give us no guides... they cannot even tell me where the feature is and how we should get to the objective. If I navigate the company without basic information, we may not even return."

This was our first tryst with battle conditions. We were given no support, no information, yet we couldn't have the Brigade complain that we were unwilling to take up a battle task. The remark made by a fellow officer, of 121 being a "honeymoon brigade" flashed through my mind but I shut it out. We were soldiers. There was a task we had been assigned and it had to be done.

MAY 17

Proud as I am, as we all are, of the institution of the armed forces, its traditions, its heritage, the *esprit de corps,* the courage and motivation of the men who serve the country so selflessly, I would still like the faceless mandarins in South Block to read the following account. It is a chronicle of 1 Naga going into action under orders from the commanders at the frontline, as also detailed in portions by its commanding officer in his AAR.

We could have driven up to Sando but the Pakistani artillery shells kept up their incessant and deadly fire, making it too risky. It took us eight hours to cover a distance of ten kilometres to Sando. Here, based on the information provided by 16 Grenadiers which had been in the area for nearly two years, we set up a 'harbour' (a sterile area concealed from enemy observation). Moving quickly in the hours of darkness, the company commanders left for a reconnaissance of Point 5100. Carrying support and personal weapons, rations which would last for at least five days and Extremely Cold Climate (ECC) sleeping bags, the 300-odd men began a dangerous journey. The climb was slow and painful. From a height of 3089 metres, they had to scale a feature, 5100 metres high. All this had to be done before dawn on May 17. And it all had to be done on foot.

A little over an hour later, as the battalion was getting ready to move, the troops came under heavy, accurate fire. According to phase one of the attack plan, the leading company was to reach the ridgeline and secure it. At 0345 hours on May 17 – barely two, two-and-a-half hours before first light – the leading company moved towards the objective. A sheer climb through cliffs and heavy snow, it was, in fact, an exercise in rock climbing. Troops were on all fours, using their hands to negotiate the steep climb. Hands that turned cold and numb as they clutched at the snow. At times, they had to put down their weapons and use entrenching tools to dig footholds into the hardened snow – a laborious, energy-sapping task.

The troops had struggled like this for ninety minutes, kneeling in the snow, rucksacks pressing down like boulders on their backs. The rucksacks contained survival rations: Pieces of high protein chocolates; *gur* and *chana* (jaggery and gram). Also, a first-aid kit, batteries for the radio sets. Agonizingly slowly, we made our way up the ridgeline. Point 5100 had to be taken and first light was approaching.

Suddenly, the enemy's medium machine guns opened up. We were caught unprepared. Panic gripped the company. The leaders tried to take higher positions, digging their shoes desperately into the snow. But the snow was like ice, hardened and slippery. Most of them came sliding down. Down to where they had begun. They tried, and tried again to gain a foothold, from two different directions this time, but to no avail. The firing was too heavy. There were no rocks, no boulders for cover. They sat in the open, their fingers crossed. Like sitting ducks.

An officer from 1 Naga told me later: "We returned fire, but firing uphill was useless. The enemy was dominating the ridgeline and had ample cover. All we could do was wait for nightfall to provide some cover. The first light of May 17 had come and gone. 'They' were still occupying our objective while we sat in the snow, the cold creeping into our bones, our minds numb with despair. We had been told it was only an observation post that the enemy had established there, with just three to four militants. That was in the briefing given to us. The firing was unexpectedly heavy. Far too heavy, for just 'four or five militants'. Moreover, they had machine guns.

The officer concluded: "As night fell, we made another attempt, this time from four different directions. The enemy fire was as heavy as before, and as deadly. We could make no progress. We were pinned down, nowhere to go. Trapped, we sat there, knowing that something was horribly wrong."

MAY 18

Back at the base camp, unaware of what fate had befallen 1 Naga, we sat down to formulate an operational plan. Tingal nallah, the stream that flows from Tiger Hill to Mushkoh village, is what we chose as our route. Arun reached Point 4460 without any mishap and radioed in saying he could see tent marks, meaning that perhaps 'they' were planning to occupy the area. He sent a patrol up some distance and since there was no exchange of fire, our conclusion naturally was that there was no one there. Not on the Southern spur of Tiger Hill at least.

Soon, we got our next set of orders. The entire battalion, except for one company, was asked to move up as well. But this time there was a different set of directions – don't use Tingal nallah. Drive up to Sando. Each company was given one map whereas each section (comprising 10 people) is supposed to have one. Maps... we had learnt not to argue about them or expect them to come to us properly marked. The terrain was not correctly outlined and at places even the Line of Control (LoC) not clearly demarcated. Getting into our vehicles we made our way towards Sando, driving through treacherous snow and slush.

Major Harpreet Singh was assigned the task of returning to base with the convoy of about 40 vehicles and his return journey was typical of the surreal state of affairs. Guiding the convoy through the snow and sleet, he came nose to nose with a convoy of sixty ammunition vehicles winding their way up the same narrow street. The driver of the lead ammunition vehicle alighted and asked, in chaste Punjabi, "Sir, *Kargil kithe hai, kini dur hai*?" (Sir, where is Kargil and how far is it?). Under normal circumstances, this would have been hilarious. Here, in the killing fields of Kargil, it was macabre. Somebody had dispatched them here, 60 vehicles carrying 105 Light Field Guns, driving through the night to an unknown destination along a one-way road on which another convoy was returning.

MAY 19

I was reminded of the experience of 1 Naga later that night on the road to Sando. First we had to cross a frozen nallah. We walked gingerly on the slippery snow. It was a struggle just to stay upright. Rucksack slung across their backs, the jawans moved, some carrying arms, others ammunition. Like 1 Naga, we had had not a single day's acclimatization and I turned around to see the men taking one step after another like robots in slow motion. They should have all been wearing snow boots.

The cold crept into our toes and pain pierced through my chest. Was it the altitude or was it guilt at having led these loyal men into hell? There they were, all walking uncomplainingly, because we officers were leading. Not knowing where they were going, they followed blindly. The sound of their feet pounding through the snow was eerie, magnified till it sounded like explosions of artillery shells.

The radio operator stopped, listened, then passed on the message to the commanding officer. The instructions had changed: We were told not to proceed to Sando. Instead, our orders were to move to *'Pariyon ka Talab'*. Our battle dictionary increased. The group was divided up. While some moved towards Point 4460 to join Arun, the others continued to plod towards the *Talab.*

I looked back. A platoon of ten jawans led by a junior commissioned officer (JCO) could walk no more. They sat down in the snow and stretched their aching legs. The tiredness creeping through their limbs, kept the cold out perhaps, as some took their shoes off and stretched out further. Some even managed to fall asleep. *Pariyon ka Talab…* the place where fairies dwell. The irony is inescapable. Everybody was numb. With the cold, with aching limbs, with negotiating narrow ridges strewn with loose boulders. We were like zombies, almost sleepwalking.

The sound of gunfire was a rude wake-up call. 'They' had probably been watching us all along, and opened up with Heavy Machine Guns (HMGs) and Medium Machine Guns. Bullets rained down on the platoon. Some of the men were still asleep. I heard the chatter of the machine guns and the screams and shouts of "*Bachao, bachao,* save us or we will all be killed!" and the JCO's voice, hysterically shrill: "My boys are dying, my boys are dying."

Our CO was some distance away, with Arun, and I could hear him shouting instructions to be relayed via radio. There was no reply. The radio operator was dead. The scene was out of Dante. The dead and the injured. One with a thigh blown off. Another with bullet wounds in his chest. Another holding a bleeding shoulder. Bleeding feet. Bleeding hands. All of them crawling in the snow, looking for shelter. Digging in the snow with their rifles and hands. Little trenches in which to find shelter from the deadly rain of steel. The CO managed to get Major Harpreet on the radio and shouted: "Quick! Hurry! Harpreet, send the mortars, send the mortars up. Prepare for cas evac (casualty evacuation)."

MAY 20

They arrived, half a day later. The men were still bleeding in the snow. The snow was slowly turning pink, then red. The firing continued. But from where? I looked up and all I could see were those barren ridgelines that extend for miles. We asked for protective fire. Over the sound of enemy gunfire, I could hear the CO screaming: "Open up the Light Machine Guns! Open up, open up!"

The guns had not been inspected. They did not fire.

Naik Harpal Singh was lying in the snow, a bullet in his chest. He couldn't crawl. He could barely breathe. He lay on his stomach, his head resting on a rock. Would he survive? When would help come? Harpal lifted his head. He was soon banging his head on the rock, in pain or frustration or anger. Or all three. We organized makeshift stretchers. But it was daylight and the injured could not be evacuated. That's what 'they' were waiting for. The chance to stop us dead in our tracks.

When would night fall? The sounds of the living and the dying continued. Wails, cries for help. Cries of "Take me back. I want to go back". Harpal wanted to go back to his wife. Back to his wife whom he had married in March. Two months before his tryst with the mountains. The bloody mountains.

The injured had stopped crawling. We placed them on a stretcher and sent them back through those mountains to the Advance Dressing Station. There again, the lack of information and seriousness was evident. There was a paucity of staff. Of blankets. We brought in sleeping bags. Naik Harpal Singh needed one. He had beaten his head on the rock too often. Hastened his death… perhaps. "Get us a chopper. Get a chopper, please. That might save his life," we pleaded. There are no choppers. "We don't fly at night," was the grim reply of a Major in the Brigade.

Later that night as I sat in my tent, I banged my fist on the ground and screamed out loud: "Rats, they are certainly not rats."

The choppers can't fly. We can't move without being killed. Convoys are getting hit, and Lt Gen Krishan Pal, Corps Commander, 15 Corps is still insisting it is a localized affair. Shells are flying in with increased ferocity. Entire villages have emptied out and yet, even now, we hear on All India Radio that Defence Minister George Fernandes has announced that the infiltrators will be thrown out in 48 hours. Is there no end to the madness? Everywhere, there are stories of fighting and soldiers dying. In Kaksar, young Lt Saurabh Kalia who took out a patrol party on May 14 has not returned. He has disappeared with the other five. Their bodies have not been found. Something is wrong. Terribly wrong.

But the top brass still mouths the same mantra: "There is some problem in Kargil." Lt Gen Krishan Pal definitely thought so and stated in a high level Unified Headquarter meeting that it was a localized affair. A localized affair? Troops were flooding the battleground, pouring in from both ends of the road – from Sonamarg to Zoji La, from Leh to Khalsi to Batalik. But Krishan Pal's assessment was that there was "no concentration of troops on Pakistani side and no battle indicators of war or even limited skirmishes."

Krishan Pal is also the security advisor to the State Chief Minister Farooq Abdullah. The Chief Minister was present at the meeting and voiced his disagreement by saying, "The recent infiltration was not a short-term plan but a sinister design of Pakistan aimed to isolate certain areas and cut off Kargil–Leh from the Valley." Farooq Abdullah was the first one to call the infiltrators "Pakistani regulars" but Krishan Pal insisted that the situation was local and that it would be defeated locally. His assessment was totally contrary to the situation on the ground. He told top security officials in Srinagar on May 19 that army convoys were moving unhindered and that soon civilian traffic would be allowed. The sense of unrealism was shocking, and it continued.

MAY 21

Blood is everywhere. Right across the stretch of about 140 km from Kaobal Gali in the Himalayan range, bordering Kupwara in the Kashmir Valley, to Batalik, Chorbat La and Turtuk in the Ladakh range. The enemy is effectively dominating the road in Mushkoh and Drass. In Kaksar, it is equally serious. The ingress has cost us heavily. He has effectively denied us observation into Pakistani territory. And in the bordering Batalik sub-sector, the infiltrators could cut off parts of Ladakh from Kargil and isolate Siachen.

The mood in our camp was a reflection of our growing unease. The bodies had been embalmed and brought back to the unit and the Granthi had offered the last prayers. There were so many formalities to complete. The doctor had to issue the death certificates, families had to be informed, bodies sent on their last journey home. The paperwork had to be completed or they wouldn't get their pension. The dinner that night – *dal,* rice and *sabzi* – tasted like cardboard.

I heard footsteps outside. The men were awake. Wondering probably, just like me, what the next day would bring. Our CO would have to speak to them, tell them that life and death was part and parcel of being a soldier. Remind them of the uniform they were wearing. Give them a lecture on the *paltan* (unit) and its *izzat* (respect).

Some eyes were questioning, some just sad. If they felt any fear, it remained locked in their hearts. If they had any questions, they remained unvoiced. "We will go up with you, sir. We will die for the battalion" was the response I knew they would give and it came as expected. Lead them and they will follow without question.

MAY 21

The mood at Brigade Headquarters had changed. Their assessments had started falling apart. That the battle to retain the heights would be daunting, even impossible, had become clearer through the experiences of 1 Naga and 8 Sikh. Down, at Brigade Headquarters, heads were shaking in disbelief. In puzzlement. They radioed instructions that were predictable: hold the ground and firm in. By now it is clear that the enemy infiltration extends four or five kilometres into our territory. They have also had time to dig in and set up reinforced bunkers. They have effectively established themselves on what the army describes as 'unheld' areas – areas unoccupied by both sides, India and Pakistan, since the 1971 war. These barren, difficult-to-negotiate mountains were considered safe from enemy intrusion. "Unheld," an officer smirked, spitting the word out. What was 121 doing? What about the aerial reconnaissance and the winter patrols?

Where were the intelligence agencies? The sleuths, who always painted grim scenarios, issuing alerts and warnings by the dozens. Brigadier Surinder Singh later said his warnings went unheeded, but then, hadn't he also told us that there were only a handful of militants? He had, in his brief to 1 Naga, specified their number: six to eight on Tololing, four to five on 5140, three to four at 5100.

But why blame only Surinder Singh? What about Maj Gen

V.S. Budhwar, GOC, 3 Division? Ask Brigadier A.N. Aul, who came in later in May as Commander, 56 Brigade to conduct operations in Drass to show you his Brigade's After Action Report if he will. It records what nobody in the army, right up to the chief, will ever tell you or show you. It says: "The intrusion was not considered a serious issue and it was felt that the intruders could be evicted with ease… On our arrival into the sector (May 22), the information available of the enemy strength and disposition was vague. The general information was that Tololing, Point 5140, 5100, 4700 and Tiger Hill were held. According to Headquarters, 3 Infantry Division, 400 to 500 militants were likely to be operating in the division sector with the majority of them being mercenaries."

Pal was still underplaying the intrusion, publicly at least. We learnt that on the telephone, in conversations with Aul and other commanders, there was urgency and tension in his voice. Read another portion of 56 Brigade's report, if you really want to know what was happening in Kargil. Look at the paragraphs that talk of Preparation and Reconnaissance: "By 21 May, 18 Grenadiers had completed its first stage of acclimatization. However, no reconnaissance could be carried out and information about the enemy was scanty. The planning, preparation, buildup and rehearsals that are so essential for an assault could not be carried out due to pressure of launching operations at the earliest." The report goes on to say: "However, the seriousness of the situation was subsequently realized with the detection of intrusion along almost all the ridgelines in the Mushkoh and Drass sectors."

It was the same story in Kaksar and Batalik. Troops were being pushed into battle, up the mountains of death. Instead of first gathering information and containing the ingress and then planning operations, we were doing it the other way round.

Launching operations straightaway. Fighting an enemy that had the distinct advantage of height. And many of us were not even trained to operate in high altitude areas.

MAY 23

We moved and set up camp near Mushkoh village. Looked for a mountain that would shield us from the shells that burst into a million splinters, taking with them arms and legs. At about 4.30 that evening, Capt Surinder Bawa, who had been attached to us as the Regimental Medical Officer, was walking towards the toilet – a hole dug in the ground and a tent thrown around it – when the shells started falling. Through a haze of dust, I could see Bawa running, the shells following. Bawa escaped but one of the shells hit our *langar* (camp kitchen). After what seemed like forever, a jawan ventured out and said, "Sir, *char ludak gaye* (four have fallen). More questions. Why is the enemy fire so accurate, so precise? Bawa was tracked as he ran. The *langar* was targeted too. Where are the observation posts? I can see nothing against the skyline. Maybe there is someone in the village directing the enemy batteries.

After reporting the casualties to the Brigade Headquarters, we sent some men to Mushkoh to investigate. The houses showed few signs of inhabitation. A few elders remained, perhaps too frail to join the others who had left. Huge padlocks were slung across most doors, some didn't need to be bolted; the roofs and walls had already caved in under the impact of splinters. The team's return coincided with another volley of shells. They were landing too close for comfort. I looked at my watch. 2130 hours. I kicked the lantern in my tent, to snuff out the light, and ran outside. Something made me turn and look back. The night was aflame. A shell had hit my tent and it was ablaze.

We moved hastily to another location to set up camp. We needed overhead protection from the shells. Their artillery was targeting us with uncanny precision. Batteries of 105mm Light Machine Guns were being pumped into the sector but we still did not have an artillery officer attached to us: An officer who could direct retaliatory fire and instill some confidence in us. Make us feel that we infantry foot soldiers are not being used as mere cannon fodder. It is getting impossible to keep the morale of the men from flagging.

We received another set of orders. Go further up on Tiger Hill from *Pariyon ka Talab.* Towards Shivling via Pathar. I received the first piece of good news. Major O.P. Mehra, an artillery officer from 315 Regiment, was being attached to our unit. We almost rejoiced. At least we will have some counter bombardment. The Pakis will get a taste of their own medicine. By noon that day, another company set off. Cutting a track through the snow they wound their way up slowly. Still at the base of Shivling, hell broke loose once again as the sound of gunfire rocked the mountains.

Mehra? Where is Mehra? He was on the radio set, shouting desperate instructions. "Tell me where the fire is coming from? Which direction did they fire from?" A feeble voice answered. It belonged to the radio operator accompanying the company commander. "My radio set is broken and I've got a bullet." Mehra: "Don't say anything, just tell me where the fire is coming from. Which side is the enemy on. Hello, hello, do you hear me, tell me please, which side is the enemy on?"

The enemy is still an invisible force. It was six o'clock in the evening and we were still trying to find out the extent of damage the enemy had caused. The company had scattered in desperate search of cover. The place where we had been ambushed is called Pathar. But there were no rocks to take cover behind. The irony was as unceasing as the enemy barrage. How many were dead? We still don't know. Time drags. The snow has turned red again. Those who could walk tried and made their way slowly towards the helipad at Pathar.

We radioed for choppers to evacuate the wounded and our spirits got a boost when we spotted one approaching. But before it could land, the shells hit the helipad. The walking wounded stared in disbelief. The pilot was brave. He hovered in the area, quickly touched ground and whisked two injured jawans to safety. He came back again, dodging the shells and evacuated some more. The final count: 12 including a JCO. But where was young Lt Tilak Bannerjee, the baby of the battalion, and three other jawans? We scoured the area but couldn't find them. Were they dead or alive?

The enemy be damned. We have to find our men. Treat the wounded and give the dead a decent funeral. The chopper couldn't evacuate all. Some had to be carried back physically. The thought of what that entailed still disturbs me. Makes me sit up in cold sweat at night. Eight men were needed for each injured soldier. A set of four could carry the stretcher and come down the treacherous mountains for no more than thirty minutes at a stretch, their shoulders aching under the weight of the makeshift stretcher, their shoes slipping and sliding in the snow.

What kind of fighting strength did that leave us with? One

third of a company, sometimes more, was required for casualty evacuation. We had been here just over a week and had already had three nasty encounters with the enemy. Four had already fallen in an artillery attack on our *langar* at base camp. And now this. Stretchers slowly weaving their way down towards the Advance Dressing Station. Six dead and so many injured and we were still searching for the enemy and their location. Where were they? How many were they?

I listened to the conversation between the wounded and the stretcher-bearers. It is testimony to their despair and frustration:

"I'll die, I'll die. *Saale,* they almost roasted us alive," groaned a voice from the stretcher. It belonged to a jawan who has suffered multiple gunshot wounds.

"Don't worry, we are almost there," replied one of the stretcher-bearers, all four of them trying to quicken their step. They had been walking for one hour and it would take another three.

"Hoya ki?" (What happened?), asked one.

"They are very well equipped and sitting very high. How will we ever reach them?"

"Did you see them?"

"Nahin yaara (No my friend), you can only hear them, their weapons," he groaned, "*Pata nahi* (don't know), where they are. How are they managing to stay in so much snow? How could they carry machine guns up these heights?"

"They must have orders too. From some *karnail, some jarnail* (some colonel, some general)."

"Theek hai (All right), we are *faujis (soldiers).* We have to fight or why are we wearing this uniform."

"I am willing to die in a war. But what kind of a war is this? We don't even know who we are fighting..."

"Why don't they fight like men, the bastards? Why can't they face us? I'll kill them, I swear I'll kill the cowards even if I have to give my own life in the process."

"My wife wrote to me. She thinks I am still in the Valley. It was Guddi's third birthday. This must be the first time I forgot my daughter's birthday. Must send a letter home."

"Will you tell them where you are?"

"I don't know. I think it is better we do. Harpal does not live far from my village and soon my family will find out that we are in Kargil."

"Maybe another unit will replace us. How many more casualties can we suffer?"

We continued the remaining two-hour walk in silence. The uncertainty of it all still gnaws at us; the question of what next and for how long throws us into spells of despair. Will we ever see our friends again? Our family?

I remember the envelope handed over to an officer just as he was moving up for an assault. Major Rajesh Adhikari of 18 Grenadiers. I saw him stuff the letter into his pocket unopened as he continued looking at the map. He was in the midst of a task and wanted to read what Kiran, his wife, had written later. 18 Grenadiers had been tasked to do what 1 Naga had earlier been briefed about – secure Tololing and Point 5140. Colonel Khushal Thakur, the CO of the unit, had had a briefing session with Brigadier Surinder Singh, and he and Adhikari were planning an operation on how to clear these features currently occupied by what Surinder Singh had said were "six to eight in number".

The next day, they had another meeting and this time Major General Budhwar had come down from Kargil. "There are only a handful of mercenaries there. There is no need to worry," he told the three COs present – Col Thakur, Col S.P. Singh of 8 Sikh, and Col Patil of 1 Naga.

We all knew what had happened to 1 Naga. 56 Brigade's After Action Report would state that their operation "did not succeed due to heavy enemy firing resulting in a number of casualties. It may be recalled that 1 Naga had been launched into operations without any acclimatization and therefore was not in a fit state to carry out operations." 18 Grenadiers was a little luckier. It had carried out its first stage of acclimatization but was given no time for any preparation or reconnaissance. Some troops from 16 Grenadiers who had been sent up to contain the ingress of the enemy had been stuck on the ridge for nearly a fortnight.

Briefed on May 21, they were asked to move the next day. Quickly establishing a base at Bimbat, Col Thakur moved up with his 2iC, Lt Col R. Vishwanathan, the Ghataks and Alpha Company. Just before last light, the same day, Thakur ordered speculative fire to engage the enemy mortars. Rocket-propelled grenades and machine guns retaliated. The weather was bad. It was raining and it started to snow. One company started to make its way forward, braving the enemy's heavy firing and advancing barely 600 to 800 yards, Capt Sachin Nimbalkar radioed his CO, Thakur, to say they were wet and freezing. They had nothing with them. No blankets, no sleeping bags.

The fog hung heavy, covering the mountains and when it lifted, the troops were barely 400 metres short of Tololing. And then, for the first time, they saw them: men in black with red headgear. About 15 of them were occupying the western side and another 15 to 20 sitting on top. The fog, suddenly dissipating, had turned the Grenadiers into sitting ducks. The enemy opened up and two men went down, bleeding profusely.

The inputs were obviously wrong. The Grenadiers had

seen more than double the number of militants the Division had briefed them about. The dilemma for their CO was acute – if the troops stayed, they ran the risk of being shot. If they withdrew, they would have lost the ground covered. Every inch was progress. A JCO, Subedar Randhir Singh, prevailed: "Sir, if we pull back, we won't even be able to come this far, unless it's foggy again."

What next? Use the 81-inch mortars and target the top. More ammunition than ten three-tonne vehicles would normally have carried had been brought up on foot. More than 70 per cent of the battalion had been busy with the task of establishing a firebase. Let it be of some use.

One of the injured, Dalip Singh, lay in the snow. He'd lost his left eye and would lie there, without help, without medical aid, without food, for probably another 48 hours. Yet, he said: "Sir, I'll come back to the fight as soon as I'm all right." Moments like these make you want to go on. Charge up the remaining 400 metres but that's what the enemy wants. 'They' were screaming *'Allah ho Akbar'* and raising their weapons in victory. Jamming our radio frequencies with similar cries of *'Allah ho Akbar'*.

Pull back. That's what the Grenadiers would have to do. But the seniors wouldn't hear of it. The COs were thinking about the safety of their men. The army brass was only interested in evicting the militants as quickly as possible, regardless of the casualties, it seems.

We had all realized by now that 'they' were no ordinary militants. Militants don't move around with Light and Medium Machine Guns. "Sir, we will push them out. But give us time. We can't promise we will reach the objective by first light tomorrow. Please try and understand the difficulties," is what I hear commanding officers say, again and again.

"Stay where you all are. We're trying to organize for helicopters mounted with Medium Machine Guns," we were told. Major Adhikari was chosen for the task of guiding the helicopter fire. He made his descent and went to Brigade Headquarters, the letter from his wife, still lying unread in his pocket. Adhikari knew these features. Men from his battalion had shed blood on them. The MMGs blazed as the helicopters circled the peaks, but it was of little effect. The enemy was too well fortified. They – the officers at Brigade and Division Headquarters – wanted the ground assault to resume soon after the air attack, but it had been a waste of time, manpower and ammunition. The artillery support that followed wasn't good enough. There were only five fire units (each unit comprises six guns) and initially there weren't even any officers in the Observation Posts (OPs) to give target coordinates and corrections.

For the enemy, Tololing was an extremely important position and he wasn't going to give up. It was at a distance of approximately five kilometres, as the crow flies, from the highway, from this vantage position at 4590 metres, that he had successfully been targeting the road at will. "It was representative of the deepest penetration made by Pakistan," 56 Brigade's report would say after the guns had fallen silent in July.

But then, even in the third week of May, who knew that the occupants were regulars, not mercenaries. That they had secure supply lines which brought them their butter and their guns. That the Pakistani Army was holding well-coordinated defences with well-sited machine guns. That they had even made effective counter-attack plans. That what Army Headquarters is at pains to call "sangars", as opposed to bunkers, could withstand our own firepower. That they had telephone lines between one bunker and another and that they had even brought up fibre glass huts to make them comfortable through rain and snow. We were beginning to see some of these signs, but what about our senior officers? They were only looking at coloured lines on maps demarcating the LoC, coloured dots for locations of features like Tololing. Here, the Grenadiers were 400 metres short of Tololing, and we were still being given a totally distorted picture of the enemy and their fortifications.

The mercenaries – that's what the Division still referred to them as – sat in sangars, safe from our artillery fire. In the cozy comfort of fibreglass huts, while we rushed men on stretchers with splinters lodged in hearts and brains. If there was a moment to shed illusions, it was now. I cried for the men. They had not just lost blood, limbs, body parts. They had lost pride. Pride in being fighting soldiers. The kind of pride only an infantryman can understand.

MAY 28

Adhikari returned to the mountains and we brought up more ammunition on the nights of May 27 and 28. Select your weapons and the timing of your attack, the Grenadiers were told. This is their version of events. Adhikari was to lead an assault on Tololing's Southern ridge. Last minute checklist. Does the rucksack have everything? A bottle of water, a medical kit, batteries, emergency rations for 72 hours. The company had chosen 0130 as its H-hour. Thirty minutes before that, the five fire units got busy. The artillery guns firing to try and soften the 'target'. The fire was aimed at unsettling the enemy and forcing him to keep his head down so our troops could move further up the mountains. Crawling inch by inch, through the snow, they tried to negotiate the jagged cliffs.

Not long after, they heard Adhikari on the radio saying he had been pinned down. Shortly after that, Adhikari's radio operator, Lance Naik Rajinder Singh, reported that Adhikari sir had been injured. "He can't move left or right. Do something to save us." Col Thakur and his 2iC Lt Col Vishwanathan rushed towards the spot. The spot where the feeble voice had breathed his last. The spot where Adhikari lay pinned to the ground. Where more had fallen asleep in sheer exhaustion and some were still crying for help.

Soon it would be daylight and that means more casualties. Sitting behind a boulder, their only protection from the havoc the night had wreaked, they heard from a Lance Naik what they had been dreading all along: Adhikari had been killed. So had Rajinder Singh, the radio operator. Many others had been injured. The Lance Naik had lifted his head to point to the place where Adhikari's body lay. A bullet had ripped through his helmet and through his skull. He had collapsed in a heap near his commanding officers.

The bodies had to be evacuated. They could see Adhikari's body from behind a boulder. So could the enemy, and the first conversation between Indian soldiers and the enemy took place that night. "If you have the guts, come and collect your officer's body," one of them said and an enraged Capt Sachin Nimbalkar replied, "You bastard, I've come to take your body."

The risk of attempting to drag Adhikari's body was too high. Thakur and Vishwanathan decided to make the boulder their home and conduct the battle from there. The morale was very low. There was no question of returning to the firebase. Or the firm-up position. It would take time. 48 hours at least. To evacuate the injured and boost the morale. For another attack. Another attempt. Instructions were radioed. One to Major Rajeev Kumar, the unit adjutant, who was at the administrative base. He had been up all night. He was already preparing to rush more ammunition. Another call. The Brigade had to be told more time was needed for the next assault. The enemy was too well entrenched. They glanced across at Adhikari. The letter from his wife Kiran lay unopened in his pocket.

The shells started raining down again, this time with increased ferocity. Then we realized why. We were just short of Tololing. Here, Pakistan had made its deepest incursion and the Brigade and Divisional Staff weren't even aware of the fact. Tololing had till then not even been identified as a danger zone. After all, according to them there were only a handful of militants. Six to eight is what Brigadier Surinder Singh had told 1 Naga. Eight to ten is what 18 Grenadiers too had been told by the Div.

We are all livid with rage. A fellow officers' body lies nearby. The enemy is taunting us, daring us to come to a fallen soldier's rescue. And all that our seniors can do is parrot the same orders: carry on and reach the objective. We are more than willing, but what is the use of just pouring troops into the mountains? Mountains which are devouring our men because the enemy is so well entrenched. Because we have been thrown into battle with no planning, no information. Or any suitable equipment. Our boys are fighting in sub-zero temperatures without sleeping bags. They will continue to brave the odds. But for how long?

We had listened to the Brigade, which kept telling us that the mercenaries were running out of ammunition. The situation on the ground was so vastly different. The enemy showed no signs of weakening. The troops knew that as well. Their faces told us that. Something had to be done. "This will happen during war," we told our boys. "We must go on. If we retreat, we will only suffer more casualties. The only way to cut our losses is to keep moving forward."

In Delhi, the people in charge, in South Block, were making a mockery of the sacrifices already made, the bodies already piling up. "The morale of the troops is very high. They are doing a splendid job. The enemy will be evicted soon," was the kind of statements our chief, General Malik and the 'respected' defence minister kept making. Morale? High? Sure. It was as high as the mountains we were trapped on.

MAY 29

The air strikes had begun. The Indian Air Force had joined the battle on May 26 and their MIGs had been pounding the heights. But even that had not made too much of a difference to the bastards. What kind of fortifications did they have? Till almost the end of May, 16 Grenadiers and 121 Brigade had been living with their families, while the Pakistanis had sneaked in, built sangars, laid communication lines, brought in heavy arms, equipped themselves with stinger missiles and even stocked themselves with dollops of honey and butter. All this we learnt later. Right now, our men were going hungry, not having tasted a hot meal for three to four days at a stretch. It is amazing what a simple, hot meal could do for the morale of the troops.

All of this had been going on, day after day, with sickening regularity, and it was not until May 26 when the MIGs appeared in the skies over Kargil that the army brass and the politicians were willing to recognize the seriousness of the war. For them, the acknowledgement came with the fighter planes and it was only then that the war got its name – Operation Vijay. But what about those gruelling days between May 4 and May 26, when we were lambs being led to slaughter?

Even the press had been kept out till May 25 when Lt Gen Krishan Pal's office consented to allow journalists in only after they had sought special permission. After they signed a form saying they were travelling at their own risk. They came in hordes, once they were allowed to cross the barricade at Sonamarg which had sealed the sector from all contact.

Finally, some questions began to be answered. Farooq Abdullah had rushed to Delhi after the Unified Headquarter Meeting when he'd spoken his mind about Pakistan's sinister game plan which he had said was aimed at cutting off Kargil–Leh from the Kashmir Valley. He had gone to Delhi on May 24 and met Prime Minister Atal Bihari Vajpayee to find to his horror that the Government of India was quite unaware of the gravity of what was unfolding on the mountainous heights in Kargil. They knew there was 'some problem'. If only they'd bothered to ask us at Tololing.

The prime minister had made his famous bus trip to Lahore only three months earlier. That had only added to the complacency. Troops along the LoC in Kashmir too had been thinned out. War was certainly not on the minds of the army commanders. Internal security duties and counter-insurgency operations were. Not one of many possible scenarios chalked out in war games had depicted a situation where Pakistan would switch from sending trained militants to sending army regulars, heavily armed, fortified, well stocked, and that too, across the heights of Kargil. In a meticulously planned operation that would remain undetected for weeks.

They had covered all the ridgelines. Fortified them with machine guns. We could not move up without incurring heavy casualties. They seemed to have thought through the finest detail. Even laid mines to hinder our movement. Sophisticated plastic mines, barely decipherable in the snow. Corrugated sheets had been brought up to cover the sangars which were then lined with more boulders. They had come in civvies (civilian clothing) and fooled the army into believing they were mercenaries.

They'd shopped well too, buying snow jackets and winter wear to survive temperatures that dipped to minus fifteen. And they'd come prepared for a long haul – with photographs of their families, envelopes to send letters in, leave applications, just the kind we have in our army. Medicines, books to read, notebooks in which their soldiers could write their own diaries. Diaries in which they found time to pen little poems.

Our senior commanders were caught napping. They had misread the situation completely. The shelling in Kargil had been increasing over the last two years. In April 1997, artillery shells had killed civilians in Kargil and it was the first time since the 1971 war that the sector had suffered civilian casualties. The following year again, the artillery guns had boomed and the casualty figure had crossed the double-digit mark. The winter of 1998 had witnessed the same pattern.

There had been other telltale signs. A Pakistani Mi-17 helicopter had flown into Indian territory in February, but commanders concluded that it had strayed into our airspace.

In October, the previous year, there was another report that Pakistan was surveying the area with Remotely Piloted Vehicles (RPVs). Scientists from the Defence Research and Development Organization (DRDO) came to Kargil after Indian soldiers reported seeing lights scanning the mountains. They wanted photographs of these lights from various angles. The army commanders, however, had concluded that the Pakistani armoury did not include RPVs that could operate in heights above 12,000 feet.

JUNE 1

I recall our own intelligence reports. The reports that were available at the very time that the intruders were putting their tactical plan into practice. These reports had been regularly reaching the Northern Command at Udhampur. MI 1 (Military Intelligence 1) specifically tasked for conventional intelligence on Pakistan, had filed 79 inputs for the period August 1998 to July 1999. Among the reports:

August 6	Northern Light Infantry (NLI) has located itself at Shaqma (opposite Bimbet in Drass) and requisitioned for civil transport.
August 11	Increased mine laying activity in Shangruti (Opp. Batalik).

September 23	Ammunition dumping going on in some gun areas. Pak artillery units being told to take pictures of target areas.
October 28	Ammunition bunkers under construction at Hassan gun position (West of Drass).

Meanwhile, 121 Brigade had the following intelligence reports:

January '98	Deployment of a few guns in the general area of Shaqma.
June '98	NLI imparting training to civilians.
August '98	Animal transport moving towards Marpola. Track improvement activity opposite Kargil and Batalik.

15 Corps had its own set of reports:

March '98	Increased vehicular and animal activity in Olthingthan.
April '98	Increased troop movement in Kargil general area.
May '98	Increased vehicular movement.
June '98	11 NLI imparting training at Kamri.
June '98	Medium guns deployed opposite Meenamarg. Two underground bunkers being constructed.
June '98	Increase in number of helicopter sorties over Shaqma. Road construction activity with the use of explosives.

July '98	Animal transport activity indicating construction of new weapon emplacement at Marpo La.
September '98	Air defence guns deployed opposite Kaksar.
November '98	Troop build up and vehicular and animal movement in areas facing Kargil and Batalik.
January '99	Increased track construction activity opposite Kargil and Batalik and an increase in troop movement.

So much specific information and yet nothing was done. No one analysed them. Why? I had inquired from a senior officer from Northern Command, and the reply had been: "But what is so unusual about these reports. There is always an increase in animal and vehicular movement when the road is open. We do our own advance winter stocking (AWS) at the same time..." This officer had come to the battleground, one of the army VIPs who flew in and out of Drass and Kargil, their visits lasting but a few hours.

JUNE 2

Up in the mountains, Colonel Thakur and Lt Col "Vishu" Vishwanathan sat behind a rock, planning their next move.

Vishu decided to lead the assault himself. He started to make his way up when it was slightly cloudy. A little later, he called to say that they were under enemy fire. Thakur turned to his radio operator, Ram Kumar, to ask Vishu for more details. To his horror, he found Ram Kumar was dead. There was even worse news. His 2iC had been hit as well. "He can't talk on the set, sir," Vishu's radio operator told Thakur. Thakur moved up. He wanted to get close to Vishu, drag him to safety. He found him barely breathing. Mumbling in pain. A bullet had hit his groin. They tried mouth-to-mouth resuscitation but it was too late. Vishu breathed his last, his head cradled in his CO's lap.

Barely a week earlier, Lt Gen Krishan Pal had launched into a tirade, even suggested to the Brigade that the CO be sacked and his 2iC take over. He was annoyed that the Grenadiers' battle for Tololing, which had started on the night of May 22, had not accomplished its task. Brigadier Aul had defended Thakur, understanding what he and his men were going through. Aware that the unit had suffered heavy casualties. Kishan Pal had called later and apologized.

But now, the 2iC lay dead. Vishu had, before they launched the final assault, spoken to Colonel Thakur about getting a satellite phone so he and the men could at least talk to their families. He was supposed to have gone on leave on June 1, and he wanted to speak to his wife. It would raise their morale. The satellite phone had arrived. But the batteries were dead. It was the ultimate irony. The cruellest of epitaphs. In these frozen heights, many more such cruel epitaphs will be written. In blood.

TWO

"Never can we, as a nation, pay you back for what you've done for us"

JUNE 1

By now, school children are flooding us with cards and letters. The Army Post Office and the Defence Ministry have decided to forward these to the soldiers in the battle zone, hoping it will serve as a morale-booster. I open one. It's written by Arjun, a ten-year-old boy from Nagpur. "To our brave brothers," he writes, "caring not for your life at the battlefield, you uphold the nation's honour every hour. Never can we, as a nation, pay you back for what you've done for us. All we can say is thanks."

I break down and cry. Not because of the letter but because of the tragic irony. If only Arjun knew what I did. That morning, one of our officers had returned from Badami Bagh in Srinagar with a shocking piece of news. He had gone to receive the dead and wounded from our unit being evacuated by helicopter from Drass, and send them onwards. The Badami Bagh cantonment borders the golf course and the officer had seen something that would have driven anyone mindless with rage. While he was receiving the bodies of soldiers killed in the war, the 15 Corps Commander, Lt Gen Krishan Pal, was inaugurating a golf championship! Krishan Pal's son, Major Neeraj Pal, an army dental officer, was participating in the competition.

I was as enraged as the officer who witnessed this scandalous event. I tried to keep it to myself. There was little point in the men knowing that their Corps Commanders were on a golf course while their fellow soldiers were dying and getting grievously wounded. Instead, I passed on the letters from the children. It lifted their morale, but only temporarily. I resolved then that Krishan Pal's action, the greatest possible insult to the men who had died, should not go unreported.

I waited at the side of the road for the first journalist to come along. They had been arriving in droves and we had read some of their reports, even though we get newspapers a week late. I spotted an Ambassador car with a press sticker on the windscreen and waved it down. The reporter was from a national newspaper. I told him about the golf tournament and asked him to verify it with his sources in Srinagar. He listened sympathetically, took furious notes and thanked me. I thanked him too, feeling a lot lighter.

I want to see it in print. I want the country to read it and feel the shock we have felt. They will see it before we do. Pal apparently felt that life should go on as normal, but what is normal about being trapped in mountains, about being killed. This is war, isn't it?

I waited with anticipation, but the story never appeared. Perhaps the reporter never filed it. Perhaps his editors decided not to carry it. The country has wrapped itself in a patriotic blanket. So, it seems, has the media. Anger is giving way to a feeling of resignation. It is the media, after all, which has taken the battle into towns and villages and given the people a sense of purpose. We all know it will not last, but passion has been whipped up and cremations of dead soldiers are drawing huge crowds.

The central and state governments are responding to the public upsurge of patriotism – giving lakhs worth of compensation to what came to be called the Kargil martyrs,

Kargil ke shaheed. Some states have given Rs 10 lakh each to the family of dead soldiers. The question of whether they would have done the same if it had not been election year keeps troubling my mind. I am sick of politicians. Sick of the army brass who are still, in the beginning of June, throwing battalion after battalion into the Kargil–Drass sector without proper equipment, proper briefings, even proper weaponry. We continue to fight against impossible odds, continue to lose brave men every day to enemy fire.

The air strikes had begun some days earlier, in the final week of May. Early morning on May 26, the message was flashed all around the mountains. Stay down, the Indian Air Force is launching air strikes on the enemy-controlled peaks. We crouched behind boulders as fighter aircraft screamed overhead and bombarded the peaks. Our spirits had lifted. At the thought of the enemy plans being unsettled. Of them running for cover. Back across the LoC into Pakistan.

But there was a problem. The bombing was not effective enough. The bombers were firing their missiles from a distance, not close enough to spot the enemy concentrations and target them. The army aviation corps had done some sorties early on and had come under fire. The enemy has Stinger missiles, capable of homing in to any aircraft that flies too close. Later, I read Brigadier Aul's report. It describes the situation quite clearly. "Air Op shoots were not effective as the pilots were not willing to take reasonable risks to go close to the Line of Control for engagement. The restricting operational factor laid down for aviation troops is seven kilometres from the Line of Control due to danger from Stinger missiles."

Then, a day later, we felt guilty for being critical of the air force. On May 27, Sqn Ldr Ajay Ahuja's MIG 27 was shot down.

He had come in close to the peaks, in desperate search for a fellow-officer, Flt Lt Nachiketa, who had been reported missing. He did not know that Nachiketa had parachuted to safety, but on the wrong side of the LoC. Had Ahuja known, he would not have circled the peaks for so long, leaving himself vulnerable to the surface-to-air missile which blew his aircraft to pieces.

We on the ground are as shaken as the officers of the Indian Air Force. We had been meeting their helicopter pilots on a regular basis. We knew from them that they were operating under tremendous restraints. A high-level meeting, chaired by Prime Minister Atal Bihari Vajpayee and Defence Minister George Fernandes, had decided that no IAF aircraft would cross the LoC. The air force chief, A.Y. Tipnis, made his displeasure apparent later at a press conference in Srinagar when he replied to a question: "The limitations were made clear to the political establishment."

We know how angry and frustrated they are. By then, they had lost another aircraft, the third in as many days. This time it was a Mi-17 helicopter, with five airmen on board. Their pilots were flying low over jagged mountains, vulnerable to the surface-to-air missiles stockpiled by the enemy. They have to fly east to west and west to east, never south to north for that would mean violating Pakistani air space. It is the kind of restriction that is carefully observed in peacetime, but generally abandoned in a conflict situation, when the enemy is located in commanding heights and inflicting deadly damage on your own troops.

Forced to fire their missiles from a minimum of seven to ten kilometers, away from the target area means a serious loss of accuracy. Sqn Ldr Ajay Ahuja paid the price. His aircraft came down on the Pakistani side of the LoC. His body was handed over to us at Post 43 on the LoC, which later became the mutually agreed upon point for the exchange of bodies, Indian and Pakistani. Later, Pakistan refused to accept the bodies of its men, a clumsy attempt to cover up the fact that it had sent in regular soldiers. But at least they gave Ajay Ahuja the honour accorded to a soldier who dies in battle. They even returned the money he had been carrying with him when he took off in his MIG from Srinagar. He'd withdrawn it from the bank to buy an air ticket for his wife, Alka, who was to join him in Srinagar.

His death has shocked the nation. It shocks us too. Shock turned to anger when we heard that Flt Lt Nachiketa had been paraded on television by Pakistan Television (PTV). Later, officers coming up from Srinagar told us the details about his staged televised appearance before he was handed over finally to the Indian embassy in Islamabad. We heard how Pakistan had tried to prove that it is India which is violating Pakistani air space. Foreign journalists were flown to the site of the crash to prove that it is India, not Pakistan, which is escalating tensions. More grisly news. The men sent to recover the bodies of the five air force personnel who died in the Mi-17 crash found them scattered all over. Eventually, iron nails and filings were stuffed into the coffins to give them weight.

However, the air strikes have brought home the indisputable fact that the infiltrators are armed with weaponry which is used to equip regular armies. Finally, two weeks after the battle has been raging, senior army officers in the field start speaking another language, telling the journalists who have congregated in hundreds, that militants don't carry machine guns and surface-to-air missiles. Soldiers do. Militants don't occupy territory. Armies do. Suddenly, it is no longer 'a localized affair'. It is a war. A war which we are still fighting with our hands tied behind our backs. A war, in which eight soldiers are needed, to carry one body.

JUNE 13

The body count is climbing, and it has already claimed some of the army's best officers. Colonel Khushal Thakur is still mourning the loss of his 2iC, the much-loved Vishu. I heard from other Grenadiers that for days, Col Thakur refused to move out, or go to the administrative base for a little rest, ignoring all such pleas that were made regularly by his adjutant, Major Rajeev Kumar. His 2iC had gone. The injured were still awaiting help. The objective had still not been cleared. Each attempt had been thwarted, each move defeated. Every step had come packaged in danger. How could he leave?

I can feel Thakur's pain. We in the army know what it means to lose your second in command, to be unable to honour the dead. We are still looking for our young lieutenant, Tilak Bannerjee who has been missing since May 21.

Colonel Thakur's grief has not been in vain. The bravery shown by Vishu and his men has pushed our troops higher up the sides of the mountain, almost in sight of the enemy bunkers at Tololing. Thakur's men are exhausted, so 18 Grenadiers has been replaced by the fresher soldiers of 2 Rajputana Rifles. Colonel Ravindranath, CO of 2 Raj Rif, led the final assault. He finally stood on Tololing and radioed Brigadier Aul to say he was on top of the objective. That 'victory' had been achieved. Back in Brigade Headquarters, officers are rejoicing. So are they at 15 Corps and Chief of Army Staff General Ved Prakash Malik's office. Point 4590 has been captured. It is the first major victory for the Indian Army.

However, Ravindranath is not rejoicing. Neither is Thakur. Thakur has already lost men, including his beloved 2iC. Ravindranath is no better off. While standing on top of Tololing, he had seen eight of his men lying around him in just about a 10-metre radius. He'd led his battalion to 'victory' but had gone back to his tent that night and wept. The loss of your men is always more overpowering than the pleasure of having performed your duty.

Elsewhere, everything seems to be conspiring against us. One of these mornings, one of my fellow officers noticed some movement on the western spur. Through his binoculars he saw about 30 men moving through the mist. Finally, he thought, they had a chance of firing at visible targets. But caution took over. Maybe they are our own troops. In the mist, it is impossible to tell. He radioed back to base and was told to hold fire. It was, he had been informed, an Indian Army patrol. After they had lowered their guns, came another message. They were not one of our patrols. It was too late. They had lost the opportunity of taking out 30-odd infiltrators. It is now early June, and we are still not clear about the location of our own troops.

Is this why I am writing this diary? It is a soldier's diary which contains not just my own thoughts and experiences, but those of all the other officers I meet in these bleak mountains. I hear first-hand details of how their commanding officers have coped with the one-sided battle conditions. This is my diary. It could have easily been Colonel Thakur's, or of one of the other officers: Bawa's, Yadav's, Patil's, S.P. Singh's, Cheema's, Nanda's, Bhalothia's, or Ravindranath's.

We feel nothing like the heroes that the Indian media is

making us out to be. Television reporters we meet tell us of the four-year-old boy lighting his father's pyre. The pyre of Sqn Ldr Ajay Ahuja. And of his young widow Alka, whispering: "I am proud of you, Ajay."

The war has inspired the nation. The media has taken the war into the private spaces of millions of homes and suddenly we have all become heroes. The names of our units are appearing in the newspapers. Overnight, we are no longer faceless men fighting a nameless war. Such reports lift our morale and ease some of the overbearing sense of futility that has engulfed us. We are not alone after all. Our effort is being recognized. We are not fighting in vain after all.

But we are still dying. Still grappling with an enemy that has all the advantages. Information is still not forthcoming. Chaos and confusion still reign. This is best illustrated by the experiences of 2 Raj Rif Col Ravindranath and his men who arrived in Sonamarg on May 29. He received the Warning Order (WO) for movement to Operation Vijay on May 25. Till February the unit had been in Gwalior. After a month's pre-induction training at the Corps Battle School at Khrew from 10 March to 10 April, the unit moved to militant-infested Kupwara for counter-insurgency operations, under 81 Mountain Brigade. Before they could settle into their counter-insurgency role came the message telling them to move to Drass in the Kargil sector. While acclimatizing at Sonamarg, Ravindranath also tried to make sense of what was happening in Kargil. His After Action Report, finally signed on September 11, tells a hair-raising story. They were trying to assess what their likely task in the war would be on the basis of 'rumours'.

Presuming that 2 Raj Rif would be used in an offensive role to evict the intruders, Ravindranath had quickly put together three teams of officers, JCOs and NCOs to work at the following:

(a) Evolve an assault methodology to be adopted for attack by the unit in view of the exposure gained by other units. Team to collect information about enemy tactic, their weapon strength and deployment. The team was told to arrive at a tactical doctrine to overpower the enemy.

(b) Assess the administrative requirements in terms of equipment and food articles.

(c) For physical fitness and acclimatization, the team was to select routes and work out a schedule so the unit could stand the stress and strain of the operations ahead.

They had heard the horrifying stories of how 1 Naga and 8 Sikh had been pushed into the mountains with no warning, acclimatization or fitness drill. The units had arrived with incomplete armouries. 2 Raj Rif was luckier. In the three and a half days between the receipt of the Warning Order and the Movement Order which came at 1400 hours on May 28, the unit had identified all items it would require for High Altitude Area (HAA) operations. Shortage of special weapons and equipment had been made up from 1/3 Gorkha Rifles and 3 Raj Rif and the unit had also carried out rehearsals in bunker bursting and section assaults.

This allowed the unit to follow the schedule worked out by the team that had been selected for the task:

Days 1-2: Normal walking on the road.

Days 3-4: Climbing gradual slopes.

Days 5-6: Climbing up to 15,000 feet without loads.

Days 7-8: Climbing up to 15,000 feet with full battle loads.

Special clothing was not available but again, they were lucky to get some items from 56 Brigade: 175 down jackets, 300 sleeping bags, 75 trousers, 50 pairs of gloves and 500 pairs of socks.

But this still left out the most crucial aspects – information and intelligence. Ravindranath did what he could do best in the timeframe available to him in terms of devising a tactical and logistical strategy. But what were they to do once they embarked on their journey into the mountains? They know, like we do, that the intruders have to be evicted, but none of us could even hazard a guess on how long that will take. All we know, and have experienced, is their firepower and its damaging effect. Their guns are lethal, their artillery precise.

Vishu died on June 2, and the following day, 2 Raj Rif was asked to prepare for operations on Tololing. The movement of 18 Grenadiers had been stalled due to heavy casualties. The Grenadiers had started operations on May 23, when it established a firm base but had been pushed back. All attempts to move North had been effectively interfered with from a feature called Hump. In all, four attempts had been made to capture Tololing through frontal assaults but were beaten back due to stiff enemy resistance.

For two days, on June 5 and 6, the 2 Raj Rif CO and his company commanders conducted a detailed reconnaissance after which they come to the conclusion that the Tololing complex could broadly be divided into four major assault areas:

(1) Tololing Top – which they decided is open to assault from the South Eastern approach;
(2) Area Flat – also to be assaulted from the South Eastern approach;
(3) Point 4590 – can be assaulted from the South Western approach; and

(4) Barbad Bunker – can be attacked from the South Western side.

The approaches had been identified but fire bases had to be stocked, arms and ammunition carried up. The bases were built at a distance of approximately 600 metres from the objective, on each axis. The last 600 metres are the most crucial, for once the troops start moving, the artillery guns have to stop firing in order to avoid shelling their own soldiers. Fire support is essential. Continuing fire, first by the artillery batteries, then using our own MMGs, Automatic Grenade Launchers (AGLs) and Rocket Launchers (RLs). This enables the troops to close in on the objective.

There are other aspects to the fire plan. In this case, it was decided to have simultaneous bombardment and direct firing followed by the attack, so as to prevent the infiltrators from regaining their balance. The purpose was to surprise the enemy by the tempo of the attack. There is no other way of surprising them. They always see us approaching. But before the attack can begin, the weapons have to be hauled up the slopes, a task which entails at least 48 hours of backbreaking work. It is decided to deploy four MMGs, two AGLs, four RLs and two 51 mm mortars on each axis.

Mules are effective up to only one-third of the route. Loading and staging points too have to be set up. Considering that the turnaround of each fighting porter includes seven gruelling hours of climbing and another four hours of descent, one porter can undertake only one trip a day. Telephone lines have to be established and ration supplies dumped. With as many as sixty porters on each axis, it takes two days for this to be accomplished. Every single item has to be thought of, including water. It is available in the *nallah* at the first staging point on each axis but has to be ferried up for the troops and that involved a daily deployment of 20 men on each axis. Men from the Corps of Signals laid the communication lines – eight kilometres of line on the southwest axis and three kilometres on the southeast as the line laid by 18 Grenadiers is already functional.

Kerosene too had to be carted up. The unit decided on 100 litres and it was ferried up on each axis by ten porters. Kerosene is important – it is needed to melt the snow and to heat up the precooked food. Medicines, life-saving drugs – they will surely be needed. And stretchers? That casualty evacuation is extremely difficult is a lesson Ravindranath has been taught before the battle commenced. Everyone knew what 18 Grenadiers had gone through and they decided to carry six stretchers up each axis. RAPs (Regimental Medical Aid Post) too were established – the closer, the better – just short of the firebases on each axis as directed by the Regimental Medical Officer. The unit had prepared for its share of casualties. Twelve stretchers were kept ready. There are other things to take care of: army mules and civil ponies were at work, so were the fighting porters. Loads of ammunition had to be dumped and the unit clerks and *dhobis* (washermen) were also pressed into action including the carpenter, Uttam Singh. He insisted on being part of the battle. Unable to see at night, Uttam Singh held on to the jacket of the man in front of him and reached the firebase, step by step. There was a complete sense of bonding. A 'will to do' and 'confidence to do' spirit pervaded the unit.

However, there was one problem troubling Ravindranath. One of his officers, a Major, was refusing to lead a company, saying he was not too well. It bothered Ravindranath, for he felt it was some sort of a sham. A sham, when young Capt Kenguruse and Capt Pravin Tomar were all fired up, more than anxious to go up there and win. It bothered him enough for him to go down to Drass, to the Brigade Headquarters, and put in a complaint.

It had to be done or it could have affected the morale of the entire unit. The other ranks look up to the officers and every move they make determines the level of trust and mutual dependency. The officers' grit, determination and leadership qualities are the key to any battle. The ranks will give everything if they see you doing the same. They will go beyond the call of duty but only if you lead. The Major said he had a pain in his joints. His men had to be reassured somehow, motivated for battle in some other way. Maybe he was actually not well. But that's for the enquiry – now in progress – to prove.

JUNE 13

The assault was planned for the night intervening June 11 and 12. The build-up was completed by June 10 and the assault companies, by the night of June 11, were in position just short of the firebase. Reserve companies were ordered to move up to the firebases by the next evening. 18 Garhwal had been asked to launch a diversionary attack on Point 5140 to engage the enemy on more than one point and divide their fighting capacity and resources. A feint attack has all the necessary backup; a sustained artillery barrage to give the impression of an impending assault. There is no actual ground movement by the troops, but it is hoped that the enemy will fall for the feint.

The feint was important. After operations by the Grenadiers on Tololing and by the Nagas on Point 5140, it was clear that the intruders were well entrenched in these places. They were, in fact, holding coordinated defences with well-sited machine guns, backed by effective counter-attack plans. Therefore a decision was taken to launch deliberate operations to capture Tololing and Point 5140 backed by adequate artillery fire support.

Then came another of those inexplicable decisions that have and will continue punctuating this battle with intervals of pure farce. June 11 was a Friday and it was felt, in the Brigade that it will give a psychological advantage to the enemy and so the assault was postponed that night. Delayed by 24 hours as it was not considered 'auspicious' to launch operations on a Friday, according to the Brigade's After Action Report. Somebody in the Brigade had clearly been watching too much cricket. Especially matches played in Sharjah. A couple of days earlier, India and Pakistan were fighting on a cricket field in England where the World Cup was being hosted and all through the game, officers in Srinagar and Kargil paced up and down. They had only one prayer on their lips: "Oh God, let India win, it will cheer up the jawans." It did. We were making little headway in our fight against the Paki intruders, but when the radio set crackled and came to life with the news that India had beaten Pakistan, a cheer went up. Spirits lifted.

But only for a while. The initial weeks of the Kargil conflict have proved to be a psychological setback and the assault on Tololing acquired crucial importance. Elsewhere, we are making little or no progress. In Drass, we are pinned down. In Mushkoh, ground assaults have not even begun. In Batalik, like Adhikari, another major, M. Saravanan of 1 Bihar is lying in the snow on a ridge called Jubar. He had climbed a rocky outcrop to get to an enemy position but his heroism was stopped by a machine gun burst on May 29. The Nagas have been called back from Point 5140 for rest and recuperation after 18 Garhwal was tasked for the feint attack.

By this time, Ravindranath was ready with his operational plans for the assault on Tololing. As many as twenty gun batteries, including Bofors guns, had been put in place. A hundred and twenty artillery guns were pressed into service simultaneously to pound enemy positions and force them to keep their heads down. Since the attack had been put off by 24 hours, the assaulting troops spent the time writing letters to their families. Many families received these letters long after they had heard about the sacrifices of their sons on television. Even before the ubiquitous telegram reached them with the official message: "The President, the Commander-in-Chief of the armed forces, regrets to inform you of the death of xxx..."

Ravindranath had hand-picked the best fighters – they were also the unit's best sportsmen and athletes – and during a little pep talk before the assault had told them that he had given them whatever they wanted and they should give him Tololing in return. A JCO, Bhanwar Singh, charged as he was like the rest of the troops, was quick in replying, telling his CO to come to Tololing the next morning. "We will be there," he had said before the companies commenced their assault to the accompaniment of "*Yeh mera India, I love my India*", a popular Hindi film song played on a mini cassette recorder.

Bhanwar Singh kept his promise. 2 Raj Rif captured Tololing after stiff battles in which they had to beat back several counter-attacks launched by the intruders, unwilling to retreat from a strategically crucial vantage point, the point where they had made the deepest incursion. A peak, from where they were targeting vehicles at will.

JUNE 13

This is a red-letter day. Ravindranath was able to go up, stand on the top and radio the Brigade Commander of the first major victory, a victory that became the psychological turning point of the war. Tololing had been taken at last. Celebrations were called for but Ravindranath wept. He had lost ten men and 25 others had been seriously wounded, including the unit doctor who now had a splinter lodged in his foot. And Bhanwar Singh, of course. He succumbed but not before he had reached the top as he had promised. They had grossly miscalculated the number of stretchers that would be needed. They had taken twelve but needed 25 for the injured and another ten for the dead.

But they won Tololing back and also counted nine enemy bodies. The rest had obviously fled, leaving behind what was the first physical proof of what the enemy had been equipped with. The reverse slopes were full of administrative bunkers which had been fortified with iron pickets and corrugated iron sheets. Approaches to each bunker had been covered by three to four MMGs firing from different positions. Our soldiers used the many tins of ghee they found on Tololing to keep themselves warm after they'd got to the top. They made a feast of the butter and honey that was there in large quantities and managed to smile in temperatures hovering between minus five and minus ten. They also found another piece of vital equipment, issued to the enemy but denied to his Indian counterpart – splinter-proof jackets. If our soldiers had been equipped with these jackets, many lives would have been saved.

Now, it is time for the post-mortem. All four companies and the reserve troops had had a harrowing time and learnt several lessons. The officers have started writing notes, listing the shortcomings and the lessons learnt. These will go into the After Action Reports of all the units that are taking part in this war. We will all make recommendations for the future. We have all learnt costly lessons. Don't ask the officers at Army Headquarters. They are busy revelling in the patriotic fervour the media has help unleash. They are playing petty games, denying that the intruders have built bunkers. Even banning the press from crossing the barricade at Sonamarg, embarrassed that the reporters are beginning to bring out the truth: no winter clothing, no snow boots. Special clothing is only one small aspect. There are so many shortcomings, numerous lessons learnt.

Here are some that are listed in the After Action Reports submitted by different units:

There was a lack of powerful binoculars required for close reconnaissance. We were unable to gather information about the objectives (the different heights which have been occupied) even after reaching as close as 600 metres because the resolution provided by the service binoculars was not sufficient.

Continuous soil erosion over a period of time had changed the configuration of the terrain. The changes had not been incorporated in maps and this led to great difficulty in identifying the routes and the objectives. Most maps had become outdated.

There weren't enough of them available and many units had to make do with Xerox copies.

Lack of night vision equipment severely hampered troop movement. The night vision equipment presently under use has a limited range and is meant for engaging targets. The units were not authorized any long-range night vision devices (NVDs) which can be used for reconnaissance and surveillance. The night vision equipment which was issued uses different types of batteries which were mostly in short supply. The result: the equipment remained unutilized.

One of the most critical shortcomings, whether in Mushkoh, Drass or Batalik, was the lack of bunker bursting equipment. The army has no dedicated weapon system for destroying concrete bunkers. Rocket launchers are ineffective. Rocket after rocket was fired but they made no difference to the enemy bunkers, solid as they were. The bunkers were made of cement and mortar. Which means that the enemy had come equipped with construction material and tools. They must have taken months to prepare these bunkers. What this implies is that the incursions were taking place even as Prime Minister Atal Bihari Vajpayee was in Lahore, on the historic bus ride on February 20.

Lack of bunker bursting weaponry: 18 Garhwal's After Action Report says that "some of the enemy bunkers had overhead protection with CGI (corrugated iron) sheets and huge boulders on top of them". The report brought out by 56 Brigade says: "The sangars proved to be very strong fortifications. Automatic Grenade Launchers, Rocket Launchers, and flame throwers had very little effect on these sangars whereby the enemy can withstand repeated attacks on his fortifications." Under 'Recommendations', the report goes on to say: "Bunker bursting capability is a very crucial aspect in gaining a foothold in mountains. Suggested equipment: Laser designators for guidance of aerial bombs accurately to the target. Cannon Launched Guided Projectiles (CLGPs) can enhance the accuracy of projectiles on targets and help in bunker bursting. Penetrating capability of flame throwers needs to be enhanced."

Milans and Faggot missiles used did not give the desired results as the life of the warheads had expired.

Intelligence gathering was almost nil. Quality air photos, which are so crucial for planning attacks at unit levels, were not available. In some cases, there was a prior aerial recce of the heights which had to be recaptured, but this was only helpful in getting a better overview. It did not help any of us either in assessing the enemy disposition or in choosing the axis on which to launch our attacks. It is difficult to plan an operation without such basics.

In Mushkoh, 79 Mountain Brigade's AAR says: "During active operations, any photo more than seven days old was found to be inaccurate." The Pakis kept changing the location of their tents, so the photographs, so important for intelligence gathering, ended up being useless pieces of bromide. In fact, the Pakis often pitched tents to fool us, for the tents were not even inhabited. It was a brilliant ploy on their part for we'd have wasted precious effort and time – planning an operation and then sending troops up heights that are eating men, tiring out the others and doing little for morale. As the brigade commander Brigadier R.K. Kakar noted, "No contact intelligence about the enemy was available. The Brigade therefore had to operate in an environment which was characterized by an information void, lack of logistical infrastructure and tenuous axis of maintenance susceptible to enemy interference."

Unit after unit was deficient in weapons. Our unit was short of machine guns. 12 JAK LI (Jammu & Kashmir Light Infantry) was short of AGLs. Supposed to be authorized with eight, it had none. The Nagas were given INSAS rifles at the last moment. 2 Raj Rif was also short of AGLs. It was given new equipment like laser ranger finders but just before the build-up for an assault. This is what the unit's CO put in his report: "Last minute issuing of equipment absolves the staff of their responsibility of sending troops fully equipped but does not increase our fighting power as there is no time for training... if infantry has to be effective, then marrying up of man and equipment must take place before the assault and the soldier must be trained in its use. The use of equipment also has to be integrated into the tactical plan or the effect of modern equipment will continue to be marginal."

The CO of 1 Naga wrote later: "Due to the deployment of the unit in counter-insurgency operations, supporting weapons have not been issued for almost a year... adequate detachments of fire support weapons are not available. Prior to induction, the unit holding of MMGs was nil and these were issued just prior to the attack. The detachment could not even fire them, which could have given them the required confidence in the weapon. Unit is issued AK 47s during counter-insurgency operations. INSAS have been issued to the unit but due to non-availability of training ammunition, weapons cannot be fired and zeroed. A large number of young soldiers were posted to the unit in CI Ops to make up strengths and were not trained in INSAS. No time was available to the unit to run any kind of cadre or to get weapons zeroed."

Lack of proper range finders: 2 Raj Rif had this to say: "Altitude affects different weapons differently. Lack of proper range table at different altitudes renders 'first salvo effectiveness' impossible. It gives away the position of our own support weapons as ranging has to be acquired through physical firing."

The effort to make up the numbers – by issuing weapons at the last minute – led to other serious problems. As Colonel Ravindranath's report points out: "The army's attempt to convert every tactic into a drill has caused a professional vacuum. Sub unit commanders were perplexed when they were in situations which did not relate to drills taught to them in schools of instruction or during training exercises. Lacking the required understanding of mechanics at their level, they tended to lose confidence in their own equipment, weapons and leadership."

Counter-bombardment by our artillery was ineffective. Ranging takes much more time than the planning figures, so the enemy got time to reorganize themselves. This compromised the security of our own troops.

Food and water were major limiting factors in the planning of operations. Lack of pre-packed meals and water added to the already high administrative burden of moving ammunition up for attack. The load carrying capacity of an individual is limited to 15 kg. In case extra weight is given, their speed of movement is drastically reduced.

Troops often went without food for more than 24 hours. Raj Rif learnt this lesson during its Tololing experience and realized that hot food for fighting troops raises the morale to a great extent. Besides, the troops located at firebase have to be sustained for over 72 hours and hence it is impractical to ferry food from the base to the roadhead. They decided then to establish a cookhouse half way to the firebase, but that meant extra time spent looking for a safe area where the shells wouldn't take a further toll. Areas were selected under cover and in the dead zone of enemy artillery fire.

After mid-June, when the snow melted, water became a major problem. Says 12 Mahar in its war summary: "The points being totally arid, even water had to be carried up. The water situation is so precarious that throughout the two months of fighting, all including officers and JCOs, holding onto captured positions, sustained themselves on barely one litre of water per day in an area where dehydration occurs rapidly due to extremely dry climate."

At one stage, all the 58 battalions involved in counter-insurgency operations had been de-inducted from Kashmir. Yet, at our individual unit levels, we struggled because fighting troops were involved in other important battle tasks like Casualty Evacuation (Cas Evac) and as fighting porters. Since Cas Evac takes place mostly on foot, it not only consumed manpower but delayed evacuation as it took eight to ten hours to bring the injured down. Then, eight to ten soldiers were required to evacuate each of the injured. This often meant that the momentum of the attack suffered due to lack of adequate fighting troops. Brigadier Kakar says in his report: "A large part of the fighting strength were employed on fighting porter duties, thus reducing the effective fighting strength. Over the arduous terrain obtaining in the brigade sector, net availability was reduced to fifty per cent as one man can carry out porter duties only on alternate days."

Casualty Evacuation whether in Mushkoh, Drass or Kargil, became a major problem. Says Brig Aul, in his report, "Cas Evac from forward locations is a tedious process and took eight to ten hours for casualties to reach the Advance Dressing Station. Cas Evac by helicopters was hampered due to enemy shelling and bad weather… The need for quick evacuation of casualties needs no emphasis. Persons with stretchers need to be earmarked for this purpose before the commencement of operations. During recce, areas of helicopter evacuation need to be identified."

The lack of Artillery Locating Radar. Around 80 per cent of casualties, fatal and non-fatal, were due to enemy shelling. So many lives could have been saved if, three years ago, Army Headquarters had gone ahead with its decision to purchase artillery locating radar. This vital piece of equipment traces the trajectory of approaching shells and calculates the location from where they have been fired. A team had visited the United States of America and almost placed an order worth Rs 200 crore. Then, the DRDO said that these could be made indigenously. But nothing happened. By the time a decision was taken on their import, the nuclear tests at Pokhran on May 11, 1998 had forced the US to impose a ban on military purchases. The non-availability of these radars was sorely felt.

The bullet-proof jackets issued for counter-insurgency operations were too cumbersome for the mountains and could not be worn because of their weight – every bit of which counts at high altitudes – and also because it is difficult to kneel and crawl forward. The jacket made movement, especially at high altitude, extremely difficult.

JUNE 14

After the capture of Tololing, which broke the myth of the enemy's invincibility, there is a marked change in the morale of our men. We have not just recovered Indian territory; the troops have won a psychological victory. But we have all paid a price. We still have no information about the whereabouts of Lt Tilak Bannerjee. Has he gone Saurabh Kalia's way? Will his mutilated body too come back in a body bag from Pakistan? How long will Major Saravanan continue to lie in the snow? One peak has been recaptured. Only one of the many heights that have been occupied is back in our hands but at least we have the satisfaction of knowing that we can do it. Despite the lack of equipment. Despite the terrain and most certainly despite the complete lack of information.

We have all been through the unenviable task of identifying bodies after they come down the mountains. The soldiers are completely out of breath. Sweating even, after the arduous journey downhill, although the rest of us have our jackets buttoned to keep out the cold. I remember noticing how carefully they put the stretchers down. One day, I stood at the roadhead, waiting for 17 bodies to come down. Register in hand, I tried to complete the formalities. Noting down names and numbers before they are put in the waiting vehicles. There are many which can't be identified, their faces mutilated. In the end, the service number has to do.

I try and recount the toll:

8 Sikh:	35 killed, 86 injured
18 Grenadiers:	34 killed, 114 wounded
12 JAK LI:	24 killed, 39 injured

And so it goes, on and on. We all sit late into the night making recommendations for bravery awards. Doctors stay up late into the night treating the injured, willing them to survive. They'd enter the makeshift hospitals purposefully, day in and day out, night after night, and emerge with their heads lowered, their clothes drenched in blood.

It is a depressing war. I often sit up late some nights and go through those letters. Take out sheaves of paper from envelopes and read what the school children have written. "Never can we pay you back for what you've done for us." I read them again and again. Look at the drawings they have taken pains to make. Drawings of soldiers standing with guns aloft. Paintings of mountains with a million flowers abloom. It cheers me, and silently saying, "Thank you too, our little friends," I turn off the lamp.

One such depressing evening, in that twilight hour, when dark shadows are chasing out the light, a journalist dropped in on us. I was curt with him at first for we have orders not to talk to the media. Have a cup of tea, I tell him. That, surely, I can do. We have not been asked to be discourteous. He tried, like all of them did, to make me talk. To persuade me to give him an inside account of the war. The questions are uncomfortable.

"How do you keep the morale up?"

"What is the enemy strength? How well armed are they?"

"The preparation must have taken them months. How come we didn't know?"

"There's been an intelligence failure, hasn't there?"

"How often have the commanders visited you in the mountains?"

"How many casualties has your unit suffered?"

There are also long moments of exhilaration. Moments in which the futility of this war does not gnaw at our insides. When we don't feel guilty about having sacrificed our own boys because our injured plead that they be allowed to battle on. At our unit, the *paltan,* bonded like one large family. Kashmir Singh. How can I forget Kashmir Singh. The valiant Sikh whose arm was sliced off by a shell that burst very close to him. He is a proud soldier.

He picked up his severed arm and continued walking. Forced on to a stretcher with his elbow still trickling blood, Kashmir Singh continued to talk. To narrate his experience with the enemy when, quite unintentionally, another soldier asked, "What is the time?" Kashmir Singh didn't flinch. "There is a watch on the arm which has been cut off. See the time there," he replied.

There are others affected in different ways. Like Capt Rajeev Kumar, staff officer to Brig Aul. He looks fine, but ask him a question and blank eyes stare back at you. He was in the Brigade Headquarters when a shrapnel hit him and he is now struggling with his memory.

12 JAK LI's Lance Naik Aashiq Hussain too has survived. A Kashmiri Muslim from Chowkibal in Kupwara, Hussain has lost his fighting arm. Torn off by another piece of a shell that found its target. He will never be able to pick up a gun again. Or go to war. He will never be an infantryman. Married in February, he returned home to his young wife, tears in his eyes. Unlike the rest of the country, where entire towns emptied out to pay the heroic survivors a visit, in Kashmir, it's not politically correct for a Kashmiri to be part of the Indian Army.

JUNE 14

Captain Rajiv and Lance Naik Hussain are only two amongst many victims. The lack of proper equipment, especially Artillery Locating radars, has seriously hampered movement.

The shells keep flying in. It eventually led to the cancellation of the prime minister's proposed visit to Matayen. The GOC 8 Div. Maj Gen Mohinder Puri takes several chances; often driving to the Brigade Headquarters at Drass – an hour's drive – when helicopters are not available. The enemy fires by day and night. They can see the road. They knew also that Prime Minister Atal Bihari Vajpayee was visiting Kargil on June 13. The visit had been well advertised in the newspapers. He was to land at the airstrip in Matayen but they had shelled the airstrip furiously, a splinter going through the well-guarded caravan that is Major General Puri's makeshift residence. Another had hit a signal's officer, Col Sudhir Bhatnagar, and sliced off his leg.

Vajpayee's visit to Matayen was cancelled and the next day, Divisional Headquarters was forced to move back towards the direction of Sonamarg, to Mughalpura, where the arching mountains assured a reasonable amount of safety. Vajpayee in fact, was not even able to leave the helipad at Kargil. He was supposed to drive towards Minjhi where civilians escaping the shelling have been relocated in makeshift tents. They never got to meet the prime minister. A handful were taken to the airstrip in Kargil and thrust before Vajpayee after which he left the war zone and flew to Srinagar for a detailed briefing at the Ops Room at 15 Corps. I wonder what the Corps Commanders told him. The truth, uncomfortable as it is? Or lies, to cover up their own lack of preparation, of anticipation, of planning for every contingency. Too many good men have died for the latter version to become the official one.

THREE

*"I am proud of my son…
He died facing the enemy"*

JUNE 13

I heard about the prime minister's visit to the Operations Room at 15 Corps. He was, from all accounts, in a sombre mood. Perhaps the intricate map covering almost an entire wall had given him a more accurate idea of the extent of the intrusion and its dangerous implications. The map would have been studded with coloured pins representing the current operational status in Kargil.

The prime minister's principal secretary Brajesh Mishra was there. So was the state governor and former RAW (Research and Analysis Wing) chief, G.C. Saxena. Shockingly, I heard that Chief Minister Farooq Abdullah had to virtually bulldoze his way in, pushing aside a captain from 15 Corps who had tried to keep the state's chief minister out of the high-level meeting.

That he had been instructed to do so is entirely possible. It highlighted another aspect of the problem in dealing with the situation in Kashmir. Lt Gen Krishan Pal is the security advisor to the chief minister, but there was actually very little that was achieved in terms of coordination with the civilian authority. The army had virtually taken over counter-insurgency operations in the state.

Though this was largely done with the blessings, even encouragement, of the Central Government, it led to a piquant situation. The army had started to look upon itself as Kashmir's saviour. The inevitable result: those in uniform tended to overlook the political system. Farooq Abdullah's administration may not be the most efficient, but he is chief minister. And that day, at the high-level briefing, attempts were made to keep him out.

What this role reversal also means is that it has left the army dangerously vulnerable in the event of a conventional conflict. Because of its dominant role in CI Ops (counter-insurgency operations) in Kashmir, the army had upgraded its role in counter-insurgency. It seemed to have become its number one priority. Most officers actually welcomed this. A CI Ops posting in the Valley ensures better career prospects for army personnel. However, the result is that it downgraded the army's conventional role and, consequently, its conventional formations and armament.

Many mechanized and armoured regiments had, over the last two years, been inducted into the Valley for counter-insurgency exposure. A lot of these troops had mothballed their equipment when they moved to the Valley. Belatedly realizing the army's vulnerability, most of the mechanized and armoured troops were ordered back to their bases.

The Kargil sector has to be cleared of the intruders but the army also has to be in a state of war-readiness elsewhere: in Punjab, Rajasthan and Gujarat. By now, the army and strategic establishment have started looking at the possibility of a larger conflict. We hear reports of artillery duels in other sectors. I, like my fellow officers in Kargil, pray this does not happen. We are poorly prepared.

In fact, to us officers, on the ground in Kargil, the questions the caretaker prime minister must have asked in the briefing room at 15 Corps were probably the same ones we are asking ourselves: how long is this war going to last? It's already been over a month since the first incursions were spotted and so far our progress has been painfully slow. And costly. Could all this have been avoided?

My mind drifts back to April that year, when the annual war games involving senior commanders were held. One of the participants was 8 Div. GOC Major General Mohinder Puri. He is camped not far from where we now are, in his field caravan. The heavy shelling has already forced the entire division under his command to move from Matayen to Mughalpura.

The war games exercises are held every year to present possible battle scenarios involving Pakistan and how to counter them. Through sand models and maps, the war games are meant to cover every eventuality. One commander is designated as *swarag* or heaven (India) while another is *narak* or hell (Pakistan). In the April exercise, held at 15 Corps headquarters, Maj Gen Puri was Redland, representing the enemy and another officer designated as Blueland represented India. Puri's main attack came from Uri and Kupwara in the Kashmir Valley. However, the presentation of one of the brigade commanders, Brig D.H. Sumanwar, involved a daring surprise attack through the areas of Kaksar and Mushkoh, the very areas from where we are all trying to evict the intruders. The aim of the war games that year at the Headquarters in Badami Bagh was to validate operational plans and readiness against the background of heightened insurgency in the Valley as well as the nuclear status of the two countries.

But in his summing-up remarks, where the corps commander gives the final assessment of the war games, Sumanwar's presentation was dismissed outright. No intrusion, it was felt, was even remotely possible through these heights since the terrain was considered too treacherous. The fact that status quo had been maintained here since the 1971 war only added to the complacency. So smug were the commanders in their analysis, even in the post-nuclear phase, that at least one post – normally occupied during winters – was also placed in the vacate category.

Maj Gen Puri must surely have recalled the exercise and realized that the intruders were already sitting in the Mushkoh area in April, the very month that such a plan was dismissed as being inconceivable. Now, it is evident to us all that the threat had been badly miscalculated. We are up against regular soldiers belonging to Pakistan's Northern Light Infantry and they have occupied the heights in large numbers.

Their strength is later put at nearly two brigades, even though initially their numbers were being estimated at 200 to 250. They have come frighteningly close to cutting off Ladakh from the Valley. Their domination of the heights overlooking the only highway made their strategy obvious: to choke off supplies to the Siachen glacier, strategically a vital advantage that India held.

That they had almost succeeded is as much a testimony to the complacency of our own political and military establishment as it is to the motivation of the enemy soldiers occupying the heights. That they are soldiers is now not in doubt. They display a determination and a mindset that defies common logic. It is almost as if they are brainwashed into believing in their own invincibility.

Once, during the air strikes, several of them died because they were out in the open. It was time for their *namaz* and they had knelt on the ground, sitting targets for our missiles. Nothing came in the way of their prayers. Not even MIG fighters. What is it that kept them going? They too are braving freezing temperatures, but then they had planned for it well in advance. We hadn't.

Yet, even in early June, when it is clear to us that the

intruders are not mercenaries but Pakistani Army regulars, Maj Gen Budhwar tells a group of us officers: "I am telling you, they are running out of steam. Just look at these intercepts, they are running out of ammunition. Go. Move ahead."

The radio intercepts from enemy transmissions he is referring to have become highly contentious among the officer ranks. Some intercepts speak of a weakening resolve. Others are voices yelling hysterically for more reserves, for medicines for their injured. Intercepts that give the impression that they are dying in large numbers… that the aerial bombings are unsettling them and forcing them to flee. That they are dangerously close to running out of ammunition, men and food.

Then it becomes apparent that a lot of this is a red herring. None of what the intercepts indicate is in evidence on the ground. Yet, it is precisely this that led to the Corps Commander throwing 18 Grenadiers into the Tololing attack. The attack in which Adhikari died and then Vishu. Move, they kept telling us, there are only a handful of mercenaries there. Go, get Point 5140, they told the Nagas and they did, only to lose many more.

JUNE 15

Right now, our main objective is to keep our soldiers motivated and their morale from flagging. Tololing is an important victory but it is only one of the features that has been cleared. Units are meeting with stiff resistance everywhere else.

The highway is still not safe and the intrusions on Tiger Hill and Point 4875 in Mushkoh are a serious headache for those involved with the task of Advance Winter Stocking (AWS).

The road, open for barely six months, provides the only way to ensure a reasonably comfortable winter – for the army and the civilians, both solely dependent on this highway for food, medicines and other vital supplies. This summer, the problem multiplies manifold. Supplies have to be stocked for all the additional troops that have been pumped into the sector.

The crucial question we all ask ourselves is: what if the war continues till October or November, when the snow will fall afresh? What will happen to us then? We will be stranded where we are, scattered at different points. What will happen to the intruders? Will they continue to occupy our territory or will the snows and avalanches force them to retreat? How many more nights will we have to spend here?

JUNE 16

Pakistan's foreign minister Sartaj Aziz has come and gone and there is no sign of a diplomatic initiative. External Affairs Minister Jaswant Singh makes it a point not to shake hands with Aziz. Only a day before Aziz's arrival, Pakistan had sent six body bags back, including that of Lt Saurabh Kalia. Did they do that on purpose? Did they time it to Aziz's arrival so there would be no headway in the dialogue?

Amidst all this, I marvel at the courage and fortitude of our soldiers, of my fellow officers. Most of them are not even trained for high altitude warfare, yet they continue to fight like tigers. Our jawans perform acts of incredible heroism despite being grievously wounded. It has nothing to do with patriotism or nationalism. We have seen our comrades die. The thirst for revenge grows stronger, but more than that, it is a sense of duty, of dignity that comes with the uniform we wear. Of *izzat*. No one will let his unit down.

Units bond like close-knit families. To civilians, it may seem strange. As for us, it often places us in unenviable situations. What do you do when an injured jawan begs not to be evacuated? Or those being treated in hospital keep asking when they can return to the battlefield. To the unit. The sense of belonging outweighs everything else.

Only our families can understand some of this unique bond. The sense of pride. The widow of an officer from 18 Grenadiers writes to Col Thakur. The letter arrives a few weeks after her husband died on this frozen wasteland. It shows how distraught she is. How her life has come to a standstill in a remote village in Uttar Pradesh. They had not been married long. But she has resolved to pick up the threads of her life, she writes, because her husband had taken a bullet in his chest. He had died, doing his duty, facing the enemy. He had died an honourable man. She is proud of her husband. They all are, wives, fathers, mothers…

Kiran Adhikari writes to the unit as well, saying she is proud of her husband's sacrifices. Scores of fathers and mothers do the same, all of them writing to us. Words that are more inspirational than all the air support in the world. Like the father of Lt Keishing Clifford Nongrum of 12 JAK LI. On hearing of his son's death on a peak in Batalik, he said: "I am proud of my son and wish to convey to everyone in his unit that they must not feel disheartened on losing their leader. They all must continue to put in their best and fight well. I am sure we will win."

The newspapers we get a week late are now full of such emotional stories. Here, in Kargil, they help us keep our sanity. Keep us motivated. We sorely need such a psychological boost. Unknown to the rest of the country, the political establishment has been pressing for proof of Pakistan Army involvement. Consequently, our senior commanders continue to put pressure on us to move our men up those deadly slopes. It increases after the victory on Tololing; the capture of Point 4590 has opened a window of hope. A strategic height has been freed of enemy control and now the commanders want us to storm more heights. To obtain proof of the presence of Pakistan Army regulars.

That is no easy task. Pakistan has been denying the involvement of its army. But for most of us, the ground situation has not altered: we are still battling with our hands tied behind our backs, with insufficient men and inadequate weapons.

Media managers in Army Headquarters are adding to the pressure. Questioning either the government or the military becomes synonymous with belittling the sacrifices of the heroes of Kargil. Any journalist asking uncomfortable questions like how, why and when the intrusion took place and why there had been an intelligence failure despite enough indications being available, is immediately being branded as unpatriotic. Worse, as being anti-national.

Yet, here we are in Kargil, sure that there has been an intelligence failure and, subsequently, a serious operational failure. That units have been thrown into battle to combat what the media managers said are a 'handful of mercenaries'. That half the injuries could have been avoided. That the army is now even involved in an intricate 'cover-up operation', all in the name of national interest.

By now, panic of exposure has set in. We receive signal after signal banning us from meeting the press. We get phone calls from the Brigade asking if any journalists have visited us. We are not allowed to give out any figures of the wounded and dead. Only Army Headquarters and 15 Corps are authorized to provide information.

I can understand why panic has set in. By now, the injured are arriving by the hour. Sometimes, choppers land at the air strip adjacent to the Forward Surgical Centre (FSC) every 15 minutes. You can see them from a distance, their rotor blades slicing through the icy winds. The sound of the rotors has become as familiar as that of artillery shells. Soon, the ambulance drivers head for the helipad on hearing the sound, waiting to transfer the wounded to the vehicles even before the chopper has landed.

Seeing the growing number of casualties, the FSC, a 25-bed hospital, now accommodates 45. In fact, even 45 beds are not enough. Some are treated inside the ambulance. Most are evacuated in Mi-17s to the Base Hospital in Srinagar after the first 48 hours. The operation theatre is in a tent where the chief surgeon, Col Anil Kayastha, works day and night to save lives, to save limbs. On 'easy' days, he operates for a minimum of 16 hours. Most days, surgery extends between 18 and 22 hours.

For the doctors and the medical staff, breakfast is a luxury. Dinner is always past midnight. Nearly two-thirds of the injured are coming to Col Kayastha. Only those wounded in Batalik are being moved to Kargil and Leh. There are other dangers as well. On the day of the prime minister's visit to the forward area, when the shelling was excessive, the FSC's operation theatre received a direct hit. Col Kayastha had to take cover in a nallah.

That same night, 17 injured soldiers, including the 8 Div officer Col Bhatnagar needed serious attention. After an SOS from us, the medical stores department at Srinagar worked all night loading life-saving drugs into trucks. Many of the injured needed blood but that is not too much of a problem, for ordnance troops are always willing. There are other volunteers too, like the truck drivers bringing army supplies. HIV kits are in place and all blood is being tested.

The medical staff, the first ones to come into contact with the injured, has sad stories to narrate. Invariably, the injured plead for their operations to be put off by a day or two. "We are very hungry. First let us eat some hot food," famished soldiers say. Often in a state of shock, most of them are physically and mentally stressed.

What the wounded can't erase from their minds are the abuses hurled at them by the enemy soldiers. They'd be taunted: "Come here, if you have drunk your mother's milk, come, come here and fight. The Indian Army is supposed to be very brave, isn't it, come and show us how brave you really are, you cowards… You will die like dogs."

That's also how quite a few are wounded. Mad with rage, they charged up the slopes, only to meet a hail of gunfire. One young soldier comes to the FSC, his body resembling a sieve – he'd taken a burst of gunfire and was lucky to make it to the FSC. But he wants to go back into the battlefield. That's all he tells the doctors, pleading constantly that they send him back. He is not the only one to express such a wish.

The staff at the FSC battles day and night, often in impossible circumstances. Like the night they had to hastily put up a tent in Mughalpura to try and resuscitate Col Bhatnagar. He had been brought in with no pulse. The medical staff pumped fluid into him and evacuated him to Srinagar at first light. His leg was amputated but he survived.

It must be some sort of a medical record – only six of the injured actually succumb during the entire eleven weeks of the war. The rest are saved. Often, the doctors would stop operating only because the generator needed to be switched off for a while, lest it break down completely.

JUNE 19

Zoji La. On the road, large convoys of army and civilian trucks await clearance to make their way to Srinagar. Zoji La is a narrow one-way pass, so traffic has to be regulated. Convoys leave early morning at six; after one pm, no movement downwards is allowed. This is the time for the convoys to come up from Sonamarg. They came regularly, carrying food, medicines, ammunition and Bofors guns. On the way back, some of them carry the dead.

A new recruit, happy to have made it to his father's unit, is going back home. He is taking his father's body with him. Another one, who had had splinters taken out of his body by Col Kayastha's able hands, is also going home. He is accompanying his brother's body.

Inside the ambulance, one of the patients being evacuated wept silently. He had been with his company commander near the top when they were close enough to engage in hand combat with the enemy. Suddenly he heard the officer shout: "Jump, get out!" Used to obeying orders, he jumped only to see his company commander's body being blown to bits. He owed his life to him; the officer had obviously seen the grenade being hurled in their direction.

Grenadier Yogendra Singh Yadav has been brought down from the heights, his shattered arm strapped to his body. Yadav had used his belt to do that. After being hit, he had hurled a grenade at the enemy post. He then rushed in, picking up an enemy weapon; his own had been lost when the bullet hit his arm. He later says he felt no pain at the time, blinded as he was with rage after seeing each of the other six members of the assault team being mowed down one by one. In that moment of madness, when fear is cast aside, he performed as if superhuman. And survived.*

So many injured, so many killed. Shattered dreams and grieving families. The numbers keep increasing under various subheads: Battle and Non-Battle Injuries (those who are wounded either due to splinters, bullets or mine blasts). And those who took ill due to the weather and developed high altitude pulmonary oedema, chilblains and frostbite. This is hardly surprising. The battleground is at 18,000 feet, the peaks icy and unfriendly.

The Medical Directorate is learning its own lessons: airborne stretchers are a must at high altitudes so is telecom equipment. Until the satellite phones arrived, information about casualties had been coming through field phones, not always reliable and limited in range.

---

* On August 15, Yadav was awarded the Param Vir Chakra.

Meanwhile, we continue to push towards our objective: Tiger Hill. We have recovered some bodies of Pakistani soldiers but the commanders want live catches; to be produced in front of the international media during the daily briefing. To be seen on television screens, much like Pakistan had done with Nachiketa.

After Tololing, the senior commanders, flush with victory, have made an outrageous demand: that we launch assaults by day. One of the commanding officers of a unit is amazed when he receives such an order. He refuses, saying that without the cover of darkness, any assault will be sheer suicide. It just shows how desperate the Indian government is to capture a Pakistani soldier alive. One commanding officer is less fortunate. He agrees to launch an assault by day and pays the inevitable price: more heavy casualties.

Yet, the demands continue to rise. Cut the supply lines, we are being told. The enemy has established a smooth network of supply lines to ensure they seldom run out of men, material and medicines. The tracer bullets fired by our MIGs had not succeeded in cutting off these lines. The Indian Air Force is flying only in daylight. The bombs falling from the skies disrupt the supply lines by day, but after sunset, they are back in business. They would work all night to keep the lines open. It is like a well-oiled machine. This is not possible unless the enemies are regular soldiers with the full logistical support of the Pakistani Army and of its chief, General Pervez Musharraf.

JUNE 20

Finally, we have got some welcome news. The diplomatic tide has started to turn. Everyone is waiting for the United States to take the lead. As it becomes clear to the rest of the world that the attack across the LoC could not but be the work of Pakistan Army regulars, the United States has started issuing a string of statements, rapping Pakistan on the knuckles. Diplomacy has started to come into play and, in these dark, deadly mountains, the fact that the diplomatic pressure on Pakistan is increasing, gives us some hope that soon all this will be over.

FOUR

"If you know the enemy and know yourself,
you need not fear the result of a hundred battles"

JUNE 26

In Delhi and other world capitals, the diplomatic war is being fiercely fought. We get the latest news from the swarms of journalists and photographers who have descended on our positions. It appears to be a paradoxical situation. A majority of countries, including the United States, have praised the Indian government for showing restraint. What this also means is that our hands are now firmly tied. The diplomatic advantage cannot be converted into a military one. There will be no question of 'hot pursuit'.

Most of the officers can appreciate that the war being fought on the diplomatic front imposes certain restraints. The India-Pakistan battle in the international arena is almost always about scoring brownie points. But for our jawans, it is a different story. We can hardly explain to a soldier who has just lost an arm or a leg that diplomacy stops him from doing what the enemy has already done: cross the LoC and defend your honour as a soldier. But the decision not to cross the LoC has been taken and a reminder to this effect is being sent out constantly to the army brass in Delhi, who, in turn, relays it to us.

Meanwhile, across these barren heights, our men repeatedly ask us the same uncomfortable question: the Pakistanis have violated the LoC, why can't we do the same? The fact is, it's a question that troubles us as well. Some officers point out the double standards. The US Army had displayed no such inhibitions in Yugoslavia. And now, the same powers are patting a grateful Indian government on the back. Beyond making an offer of providing winter clothing and specialized mountaineering equipment, America's main interest is increasingly clear, even to us in the battlefield. Which is to portray itself as a global policeman-cum-peacemaker. Thus, Nawaz Sharif is eventually dragged to Washington. An unequal war is being waged in the mountains of Kargil but in the corridors of South Block, political and diplomatic architects are busy drawing up a blueprint for a negotiated settlement.

None of us wants this battle to end now that we are finally gaining an edge over the enemy. We need to clear them out of our territory before our jawans can even start to think about this war ending. For them, the enemy has invaded the country and killed their comrades and, in some cases, family members. The desire for revenge is so powerful you can almost feel it. You can certainly hear it.

I did one morning at the airstrip next to the FSC. One of my jawans was there. He had accompanied some injured soldiers to Gumri and is overcome by the sight of choppers flying in with the wounded. Or flying out with the dead. A photographer from a Delhi-based magazine was also there, taking pictures of the injured and the row of coffins. It would become a familiar sight in most newspapers, of officers and fellow soldiers saluting the dead as they leave on their final journey home.

Home. Inside a hospital tent, one of the wounded soldiers was telling the photographer he wanted to go home, but not while the rest of his unit was still fighting in the mountains. "Yes, I constantly think of my family and when I miss them, I look at their photographs. I long for home but the country comes first." The jawan from my unit overheard the conversation, and couldn't control his emotions. He strode up to the photographer and said: "How many more do they want killed? If they don't let us cross the LoC, there will be no end to this. If the Pakis don't kill us, soon the snow will. What has happened to the *greh mantri* (home minister)? He had talked of hot pursuit. What better chance will there be? It is our legitimate right to carry the battle into their territory…"

Then he stopped and abruptly left the tent, as if ashamed by his outburst. Especially since he knew that I was nearby and may have overheard him. I hadn't, but later I met the photographer who told me what the jawan had said. I silently sympathized. One of the officers from my unit had been in Srinagar the day the prime minister had given a press conference on his way back from Kargil. The prime minister had avoided answering questions on whether the war would be taken across the borders and whether the nuclear tests at Pokhran had ended up blunting India's conventional superiority.

JUNE 28

The diplomatic moves for a negotiated settlement are adding more urgency to our attempts to clear the heights. Tololing has been taken, and it has taught us some valuable lessons. We now have a better idea of what we are up against. It's not just the fanaticism of the enemy or their numbers. We can deal with that.

Indeed, we are trained to deal with that every day of our lives. Here, in these mountains, is something we have never faced before. The weather saps our strength. The treacherous terrain finishes the job. So many soldiers have died while clinging to a rock face, within reach of the top, only to face a barrage of boulders which would send them crashing to the ground below. To die like this, killed by a boulder thrown by an unseen enemy, is, for any soldier, an ignominious way to die.

We are beginning to think positively. Tololing has taught us that the peaks can be vacated and recaptured. So, we officers are determined not to repeat the experiences of the Grenadiers and the Nagas. The major operations in the Drass sector at this time are targeted at Three Pimple and Point 4700. Two units, 2 Rajputana Rifles and 18 Garhwal Rifles are tasked for these enemy positions. Three Pimple Ridge (so named because it consisted of three hillocks resembling pimples) emanates from Point 5100 on the Marpo La ridgeline to the west of Tololing *nallah.* Bifurcating into two ridgelines at another point called Junco, one ridge branches off towards Point 4700. The feature effectively dominates not just the national highway but Drass town and Sando Valley.

Capturing these points is vital. It will pave the way for attacks on Point 5100 and Point 5060, after which the area east of Sando nallah in the Drass sector will be free of enemy intrusion. Simultaneous attacks on Point 4700 and Three Pimple have been planned tonight, along with a feint attack from the South, towards Junco, by 16 Grenadiers. The two units must be undergoing the same gruelling drill of building up logistics: stocking up arms and ammunition, of porters ferrying food supplies, kerosene oil and medicines. The snow is beginning to melt, so even water must be being taken up. And the stretchers, of course, to evacuate the injured and the dead. Rajputana Rifles has already learnt its lessons on this one.

JUNE 29

Our artillery guns started to pound the targets at the appointed time: 1800 hours. The deep boom of the Bofors guns echoed through the peaks as they softened up Three Pimple with a continuous barrage. The enemy, having the advantage of height, returned the artillery fire, targeting troops of 2 Rajputana Rifles which were firming up for the attack. Even before Raj Rif could launch the assault, they suffered two casualties. But by 2030 hours, the assault on Knoll was under way and the attacking company even managed to capture one bunker, but at a huge price: the company commander and the second in command were both killed. Headless after these early reverses, the attack was temporarily halted. The Bofors, which proved to be a winning factor in the Kargil operations, was put into action again and the attack continues. I am still awake. By 0330, our radio operator conveys some morale-boosting news: Knoll has been captured.

Our radio sets are crackling almost constantly now with sounds of the battle and reports of our progress. Another company has made its way to Lone Hill, also a part of the Three Pimple feature. The company did what most of us tried to do during assaults: choose the most difficult approach, so there is an element of surprise. But this also means climbing mountains at gradients of 80 degrees and above. This company did just that by taking the Northern approach and was able to close within 200 metres of Lone Hill without being detected. They come under heavy automatic fire and had no option but to withdraw to the fire base. It is a hellish night as the battle rages through the dark, eerie hours.

JUNE 30

Finally, we hear the news we have all been waiting for. Three Pimples is secure. Another feature is back in Indian hands. The same day, troops belonging to 18 Garhwal Rifles pressed home their attack, despite taking heavy casualties, and another obscure height on the map – Point 4700 – has also been cleared. 2 Rajputana Rifles lost three officers including Major P. Acharya, whose young wife is carrying their first child. Ten jawans lie dead and 52 are injured. 18 Garhwal too has its dead to mourn and it's injured to evacuate. Together, the two units suffer a total of 29 dead and as many as 75 are left battling for their lives. Those injured in the early hours of June 29 had to be evacuated and the effort of carrying them downhill takes more than a day. The last one reaches the Advance Dressing Station at Drass at 1500 hours, the next afternoon.

The casualties suffered by Rajputana Rifles and 18 Garhwal Rifles have been particularly heavy. Most of us believe it is because June 27 was a full moon night and it lit up the peaks, making concealment difficult. We didn't have night vision devices. Our binoculars were far from useful at night. We should have been happy to have some sort of light. It helped the troops make their way up the mountains. But it also gave us away.

However, this happens in all battles. A disadvantage for one element in the battle is actually an advantage for another. The full moon and its onset encouraged the Indian Air Force to strike at night. The idea: unsettle the intruders and don't let them sleep either by day or by night. Let them also be on their toes. That way, they might tire. It also encouraged the pilots to fly lower. By now, Mirage 2000s have been inducted; their laser-guided bombs doing a better job of hitting desired targets, even bursting open sangars. Equipped with electronic warfare packages, Mirages are also able to jam radar guided Surface to Air Missiles. A Pakistani supply camp at Manthodalo in the Batalik sector has blown up in one such attack, a cluster of buildings pulverized in the process.

JUNE 30

Successes are finally coming our way, even though several peaks still remain in Pakistani hands. However, one point is now clear: the intruders are no longer invincible. Yes, they are still a tough enemy capable of inflicting heavy casualties. They are still launching counter-attacks and not running away from the battlefield, as our spokesperson in Delhi often liked to say. In fact, 2 Rajputana Rifles has lost 13 of its men and recovered nine Pakistani bodies in return. That gives some idea of the odds our men are fighting against and the enemy's decisive advantage of height. They are also well stocked and well equipped for this battle in the mountains. Yes, much better equipped than we are.

Take the recoveries from Point 4700 for instance. 18 Garhwal was able to take stock of those today. The Pakistanis are not going hungry like we were. A *langar* with huge quantities of rations that could last the intruders for at least 30 days was destroyed by 18 Garhwal. That's how well stocked they were. It's no joke, as any of us will tell you, carrying such huge quantities up those heights. They had obviously taken their time, building up bit by bit and preparing for what they clearly thought would be a long haul.

The Garhwal unit's After Action Report, in fact, said: "The enemy had prepared defences over a period of time. All approaches leading to the heights had been covered by fire. Some of the bunkers had overhead protection with CGI sheets and huge boulders on top of them. They were well stocked with weapons and ammunition. The ammunition recovered could have well lasted them for a month if they had decided to fight it out. They had adequate snow clothing and equipment and adequate rations to last a month."

Such discoveries become more frequent as the battle progresses and we start to clear out the intruders. Clearly, strategies have to be revised. What would in a conventional war, require one or two fire units, now requires double, even triple that number. Point 5140 which finally came back to us required the involvement of five different infantry units. The task had initially been designated to 1 Naga. That is the kind of overwhelming numerical superiority we need to clear these peaks of the enemy.

Superstition continues to play a role in strategic decisions. 56 Brigade and 8 Division had, as I wrote earlier in this diary, postponed its attack on Tololing by a day because they believed Fridays gave the Pakistanis a psychological advantage. The Sharjah Syndrome it is called. After the capture of Tololing, all major operations were launched on Saturdays, including the one on Tiger Hill, which along with Tololing, has become a household name all over the country. But long before the final assault on Tiger Hill, there are other features that have to be cleared. And we are still being asked for live proof of Pakistan Army involvement.

We have their dead. And a head. The experiences of 18 Garhwal also show another side of the war. The frustration that has built up among our jawans and the thirst for revenge. Having captured Point 4700, not without significant casualties, their jawans went berserk. One of them took out his knife and slit the head of a Pakistani soldier in one stroke. The head was sent down to the Brigade Headquarters at Drass and pinned to a tree trunk. None of the enemy has yet been captured alive – but this is proof that it is only a matter of time.

The enemy head, a grisly trophy, became an exhibition piece. Maj Gen Puri came down from Mughalpura to see it. Other officers dropped in to Brigade Headquarters to take a look. So did some of the journalists who have been routinely visiting the Brigade Headquarters. It was there, pinned on the tree, for anyone who could bear to look at it. In fact, the reporters were always shown the head with the warning that they won't be able to sleep for the next three nights. The sight of the pinched face, hair intact, served the macabre purpose of motivating the troops. Or at least, that's what some brigade officers believed. To be honest, it did. This is the first time we have laid our hands on the enemy. We have killed one of them. The sight of the head pinned on a tree has a salutary effect. In a way, it makes us feel better. The enemy is no longer invisible. Or invincible. It hangs there for a couple of days before Maj Gen Puri asks for it to be removed, after which it is buried in a corner.

Our string of successes has raised the morale of the men, sorely needed now that the course of the battle has started to turn. Every success now carries its own omen, for good luck. One of the commanding officers heard about the clearing of Point 4700 on his radio set. Around the same moment, he spotted a mountain goat close to their base camp. He immediately stopped his jeep and brought her to the camp. He had found his unit a lucky mascot, alive this time. He named her Tingalee, after Tingal *nallah.* She became the unit mascot and strict instructions were issued that she is not to be touched: jawans will do anything for a good meal. Tingalee survives and accompanies the unit on all of its moves.

JUNE 31

We are on the move again. We hear that there is a major offensive being planned, presumably on Tiger Hill. In psychological terms, it will be a prize target. We are now eight weeks into the battle and better prepared – mentally and physically. The successes of Tololing, Knoll and Point 4700 have given us a fighting edge. Those peaks no longer look so forbidding and deadly. Here, I am reminded of a quotation from the ancient Chinese general and strategist Sun Tzu, read avidly by armies all over the world, who wrote over 2500 years ago: "If you know the enemy and know yourself, you need not fear the result of a hundred battles. If you know yourself but not the enemy, for every victory gained you will also suffer a defeat. If you know neither the enemy nor yourself, you will succumb in every battle..."

FIVE

"If you can, please come and see where the Indian Army fought for your tomorrow"

JULY 4

My unit is amongst those involved in the assault on Tiger Hill. Capturing this conical feature will represent, even more than Tololing, the biggest psychological and strategic victory of the war. Perhaps the name has something to do with the stature and publicity it has received. It will also be one of the fiercest battles in the Kargil operations. The enemy too knows the psychological importance of Tiger Hill. Certainly, they will fight like tigers to retain it, of that we have no doubt. But even while our men were in the midst of this battle, in one of those bizarre interludes which our politicians never fail to provide, the Defence Minister George Fernandes, announced the capture of Tiger Hill.

We heard of this later, but when the announcement was made, the peak, Tiger Top, was still in the hands of the enemy. The peak had not been recaptured. The troops of 18 Grenadiers – tasked to capture the top – were still short of the pinnacle. Two courageous young officers, Lt Balwan and Capt Sachin Nimbalkar, were at that very time making repeated attempts to dislodge the intruders from Tiger Top. They were still 50 metres short of the peak when the message was conveyed to Brigade Headquarters: they are short of the top. The message went up the line, through Srinagar and Udhampur to Delhi. Somewhere along the way, it became, "They are on Tiger Top". The defence minister was told of this 'great victory' while he was addressing a public meeting in Punjab.

Such public gaffes are the least of our worries. Up on these treacherous slopes leading to Tiger Top, the battle still rages. The unit, after a recce, decided to go up the eastern slope. In sections, this meant a gradient of 90 degrees – a steep, almost impossible climb. But it was the only way we could induce some element of surprise into the attack. Troops had left the firm base at 2000 hours the previous night, and by 1100 hours the next morning, they were just short of the top. All night they had struggled up the slope, using ropes in places to haul the troops forward. The guns had to be tied to their backs.

They reached a stage when they were too close to avoid being detected. Enemy gunfire raked the slopes and the boys were forced to retreat, carrying two injured soldiers: one with a bullet in his chest and another with splinter injuries. Boulders and stones came hurtling down when the company commander give instructions for the soldiers to pull back. Try again. But not now. The decision was to wait for nightfall and then make a second attempt.

This time, the lead assault party consisted of six soldiers led by Yoginder Singh Yadav. Again, they reached barely fifty metres short of the top, hanging precariously to one side of the cliff. Craning their necks, they could see six of the intruders. The intruders had spotted our troops as well and had immediately opened fire. Soon a cloud of smoke cut them off from the top. They couldn't see what was happening, but could hear the thump of Rocket Propelled Grenades (RPGs) being used by the enemy.

Of the six soldiers who were in front, only one survived but he had taken seven bullets. Yoginder Singh Yadav, who tied his broken arm to his belt, continued firing. The enemy, however, stopped firing but the smoke was so thick that it was impossible to see anything. Instead, they reverted to their familiar strategy of throwing boulders to dislodge us from our positions on the rock face. Each one of the troops had been hit by falling boulders, their helmets and pure luck keeping their heads from being smashed open. They all ducked or found cover and radioed for what we call 'save our soul fire', an artillery barrage from our long-range Bofors guns. It's a risky call: the shells exploded a few metres away from us. It provided the necessary covering fire for them to pull back and take stock of the casualties.

JULY 6

We had carried food for 72 hours comprising *puris, sabzi* and boiled eggs but soon that was in short supply. Sachin had taken up several packets of cigarettes and he was almost chain smoking. It helped him keep awake. Close to 72 hours, and none of them had taken a minute's rest. The enemy was above us, and the recapture of Tiger Hill our priority. In a few hours, there was no food left. The radio messages had been urging us on getting more frantic and frequent. We realized why: news of the statement issued by the defence minister had reached Brigade Headquarters. Our senior officers wanted the Indian flag to be hoisted on Tiger Top, no matter what the cost. The world had already been told that it is back in Indian hands.

The third assault began. Another company from 18

Grenadiers moved up towards a feature called Collar. That move forced the intruders on top to divide themselves up to defend their positions. It was what we had been waiting for. They moved up the slopes again, with 23-year-old Nimbalkar having suddenly turned religious, muttering prayers for their success. Nimbalkar – codenamed Sholapur, after the town in Maharashtra he comes from – led the assault. He was within earshot of the abuses and threats being hurled at them by the Pakistanis. "You bastards, come on up, we'll teach you a lesson, you sons of bitches ..." they had taunted.

Their forces were now spread out, with some of them having moved to defend Collar. They were not really expecting a third attempt so soon. Not after the damage inflicted by the boulders they had hurled on us a short while earlier. Nimbalkar led, he knew the route so well; he'd been up and down twice. His men were able to approach the top with minimum noise and the silence of their assault had taken the enemy by surprise. Within minutes, they captured the first of the seven or eight bunkers located on Tiger Hill.

The assault team stormed the bunkers. We were too close to the enemy for anything but a hand-to-hand combat. There is no advantage of height now. It's every man for himself. Man to Man. Our jawans fought like men possessed. The sounds of close quarter battle – the screams, the shouts, the curses, the gunfire, grenades exploding – had all blotted out as the troops focused on their immediate task: to evict the enemy from Tiger Hill. By 0130, after what seemed like hours of fierce fighting, Tiger Top was ours. But not Tiger Hill. Portions of it were still occupied by the enemy.

The troops heard the echo of cheers from down below. The radio operator had conveyed the news of the victory. There would be no embarrassment for the defence minister now. But we were too exhausted and relieved to care. Or sleep. Instead, soldiers started examining the ammunition dump the Pakis had carried up the heights. It sent a shiver down our spines. The quantity of arms and ammunition was awesome. It could have lasted the enemy another few weeks. The heavy weapons, including Light Infantry Guns weighing over a 1000 kg, could only have come up by helicopter. The planning and effort required for all this left us with no lingering doubts. This was a Pakistani Army operation, from start to finish.

JULY 7

The battle against the last remaining resistance on Tiger Hill still rages. The sounds of battle continue on the other side of Tiger Hill, where Major Harpreet and his men are meeting with stiff resistance from the enemy. He had, in fact, been caught in the middle at a point named Helmet. The intruders from Tiger Top who had moved towards Collar, had pinned him down from one side, with the remaining enemy force firing at him from the feature we had named India Gate.

One of the heaviest firefights of Operation Vijay ensued, with Harpreet and his company putting their rocket launchers to maximum effect. Harpreet had radioed a message saying it was difficult for them to survive. There was nowhere to hide. No boulders behind which to crouch; to take some sort of shelter. They had to innovate and they did. They picked up ten Pakistanis they had killed and used the bodies as a human shield, screaming, "Come shoot your own men!" as they charged forward. This was one of the most crucial assaults of the entire war. They had to keep the momentum of the assault going. To stop now would have given the enemy a chance to regroup. Finally, as dusk started to fall in the mountains, the last intruder fled. Tiger Hill was ours, the Indian tricolour flapping in the icy wind.

JULY 8

We are numb and exhausted, too exhausted even to sleep. Or rejoice. There will be no celebrations for us up here. Too many of our men have given their lives to retake barren pieces of land. The morning dawned on soldiers sprawled out across the feature. Some were completely exhausted, lying there with eyes wide open, unable to sleep. The rest were dead. Lt Balwan was in a daze. When he had set off for the assault, he had 20 soldiers. Now only two are still alive.

Below, the commanders are rejoicing. The taking of Tiger Hill was one reason. Now, it appears they had another. We got the story later from our fellow officers, that from Batalik, two days before we began our final assault on Tiger Hill, the first enemy soldier had been taken alive. He was captured by 12 JAK Light Infantry. His name is Inayat Ali and his passbook and other papers identified him as belonging to the Northern Light Infantry battalion based in Skardu. The flurry of frantic activity his capture unleashed is unbelievable. Senior officers in the Military Intelligence (MI) Directorate and Military Operations called every hour. They were in a hurry to lay their hands on the prize. "Get him, bring him down… airlift him. Just send him. Make sure there is no firing." The messages came thick and fast. Ali was their proof of Pakistani involvement. The biggest catch of the war. The diplomatic value would be priceless. They are so keen that he arrives safely that, incredibly, the generals even agreed to temporarily suspend operations. So long as Ali was dispatched to them alive, in one piece.

A special helicopter was arranged for him and, under heavy guard, he was brought down to the helipad. Throughout the six hours it took to bring him down the mountain, the frantic calls kept coming. Army Headquarters were monitoring his position almost step by step. His photographs needed to be splashed across the world. There was also the interrogation that would provide the answer to those vital questions: When did he first set foot on Indian soil? When did the first intrusion take place? What equipment was issued to them and by whom? How many other regular army battalions were involved?

My fellow officers in the Batalik sector already know the answers. They had accompanied Ali down the mountain and he had told them, while scrambling down, that he had crossed over into Batalik way back in November! He thought some others had crossed over even earlier. They needed to be in position before the snow came, so they could find the rocks and boulders they used to construct their bunkers. After November, this area is covered in at least twenty feet of snow.

This gave lie to the official version being put out by the defence ministry and the army spokesmen, that the intrusions had taken place in April. It suited the army brass and the government to stick to the story. The Opposition parties, we read in the papers, had been asking uncomfortable questions; accusing the government of having gone to Lahore at a time when the Pakistani Army had already occupied Indian territory.

Up here, we are starting to get the real story. By now, we have cleared enough of their positions to make an analysis of what they had left behind while fleeing. We have a bagful of documents: soldier's pay books, register entries, leave slips and personal diaries that give detailed accounts of the intrusion, the identity of the intruders, and their instructions. We also have their weapons with markings and numbers of the army units to which they belonged.

Reading the personal diaries of the Paki soldiers gave us a strange sort of satisfaction for they wrote of the hardships they had faced. But they also tell how they had been sitting on those heights for months and how the operation had been planned long before Prime Minister Vajpayee's bus rode into Lahore. Long before the handshakes and the warm embraces. We found scores of letters the Pakistani NLI soldiers received from their families that date back to August 1998. Lt Muhammad Maaz Ullah Khan, a young Pakistani soldier of the 8 Northern Light Infantry (NLI), whose personal diary was recovered from Point 4812, had left for Kargil from Rawalpindi as early as January 1, 1999. Interestingly, he began his diary with a verse from Ghalib: *"Ragon mein daurte phirne ke hum nahin kayal, Jo aankh se na tapka woh lahu kya hai..."*

The extracts of Lt Maaz Ullah Khan's personal diary (see annexure) prove, beyond any shadow of doubt, that the Pakistani Army had put its Kargil plan into action well before the year 1999 started. Lt Maaz Ullah was in only one of the NLI units which reached the LoC in early February – well before the Lahore bus journey made by the prime minister.

More shocking is the discovery that the Pakistani army chief, General Pervez Musharraf, had actually visited Mushkoh. The man who planned and set in motion the intrusion was actually on Indian soil! This was revealed in another personal diary, written by Capt Hussain Ahmad and recovered from a bunker in Mushkoh. According to the diary, he came to Hussain post, located on Point 4815 in Mushkoh on February 7, 1999. Posted from 17 Frontier Force to 12 NLI, Capt Ahmad (I-card no: 064394) lists his CO's name – Lt Col Syed Ahmad Bashir – and talks of the Pak Army Chief Pervez Musharraf's visit to Mushkoh.

Even more incredible, he reveals that a Pakistan Mi-17 entered Indian territory to airdrop supplies for the intruders about the same time the two prime ministers were locked in an embrace at Lahore. The diary shows that Capt Ahmad and his colleagues began to establish posts in Mushkoh right from February onward; undetected by the Indian Army's aviation wing which often flew over the mountains for aerial surveillance. I remember Brigadier Surinder Singh had asked for a surveillance aircraft to be parked at Kargil but his request had been rejected. Still, 121 Brigade had done close to 120 hours of flying time over the area, during which they obviously failed to pick up any sign of the intruders or their bunkers.

The documents we have captured now spell out the full story. The main invading force had come from four Northern Light Infantry battalions and two companies of the Special Services Group under the Force Commander Northern Area (FNCA). The regular army battalions were 4 NLI based in Gilgit, 6 NLI located at Skardu, 5 NLI based in Minimarg and the Dansam-based 3 Northern Light Infantry. The force was approximately two Brigades strong, supplemented by Mujahideen from the Lashkar-e-Taiba, Harkat-ul-Ansar and a sprinkling of veterans from the Afghan war. An additional brigade had been moved into the FCNA as reserves.

Pakistan had based its strategy on very simple logic: that we had given up the peaks as insurmountable. That our seniors, caught in a counter-insurgency mindset, had not imagined that Pakistan would push in people in a predominantly Shia-inhabited area. They had expected infiltrators to sneak in through the Valley and through Rajouri and Poonch, but not for a minute had they thought this was likely from the Kargil sector. This had already been discounted during the war games in April.

The strategic aim was equally obvious: secure dominating heights on the Srinagar–Leh road, cutting off Ladakh from the Valley. The intrusion would alter the status of the LoC and give Pakistan control over a significant and strategically vital piece of Indian territory. Tactically, it was a perfectly planned operation. But it did not account for one crucial factor: that the snows would melt early. It is sheer providence that a weak winter saw the Zoji La pass open in early May instead of in mid-June. That was how the intruders were discovered.

JULY 10

On one of his helicopter trips to Kargil, the Army Chief General Malik asked one of the officers accompanying him to collect all the documents we had recovered and load the bag into their chopper. "It's not that we want to hide anything, but MI (Military Intelligence) will do a good job of analyzing them," he had said. We officers know that MI had been caught napping; their intelligence inputs had made no mention of a possible intrusion in the Kargil–Drass sector. We had heard reports way back in 1998 of Pakistan having constructed an Advance Landing Ground (ALG) at Deosai Plain. No one in MI gave it much credibility. It was from the ALG that rations, ammunition, men and weapons had been airlifted and dropped off on the heights where they had ultimately set up bunkers and positioned their guns.

It is not surprising, is it, that many of our officers and jawans, knowing what awaited them up on those deadly peaks, had gone up knowing they would not be coming back? Capt Vijayant Thapar was one of them. He had written to his family shortly before he left for the fight for Three Pimples. "Dear Papa and Mama," he wrote, "By the time you get this letter, I'll be observing you all from the sky, enjoying the hospitality of *apsaras*. I have no regrets. In fact, even if I became human again, I'll join the army and fight for the nation. If you can, please come and see where the Indian Army fought for your tomorrow… never forget the sacrifice of these men. Papa, you should feel proud. Mama, so should you… OK then, it's time for me to join my clan of the Dirty Dozen. My assault party has 12 chaps… Best of luck to you all… Live Life Kingsize."*

**Author's insertion*: After the war was over, Vijayant's father kept his son's last wish and came to the mountains to see where Vijayant – codenamed Arjun for the assault on Three Pimples – had given himself for the nation, fighting even after he had been hit. His heroism, and that of his number two, Subedar Shiv Naik, is not without reward. Three Pimples was taken that night.

I recall reading another letter, written by Lt Neikezhakuo Kenguruse – Neibu to his friends. Neibu had written to his friends at the Government High School in Kohima, wishing them the best of luck for their examinations. In the letter, he talked about the men under his command and their cheerfulness in going into battle. Two weeks after he wrote the letter, Neibu was dead. We collected the personal effects of the slain jawans. Most had gone into battle carrying photographs of their families. Some carried letters and postcards with heart-rending messages from little children. *"Dushman ko maar ke aana" (do kill the enemy)* and "Papa, *jeet ke aana"* (come back victorious).

Battalion commanders had gathered to compare notes later in the evening. A commander couldn't believe that while soldiers from the holding unit were enjoying the company of their families who had come up to spend the summer vacations, the intruders had already ensconced themselves on the heights of Kargil. In fact, the Director General Military Intelligence had visited Kargil on May 5 and had not mentioned a word about the intrusion. It was the same day an Indian Army patrol had been ambushed.

As a face-saving measure, some heads have rolled. Brigadier Surinder Singh, commander of the independent 121 Brigade based at Kargil, was removed from the sector for operational reasons. He was sent off in mid-June, along with Col Pushpinder Oberoi, the commanding officer of 16 Grenadiers. Tell me, were they the only ones at fault? How could our intelligence have been so poor? What about all our commanders who had been equally ignorant about the extent of the infiltration? What about all those who are dead and wounded? Who is responsible for them?

JULY 11

My diary is almost full. I'll have to lay my hands on another one. Hopefully, the war will not last too long, and it may not be needed. We read in our week-old papers that Pakistani Prime Minister Nawaz Sharif had flown to Washington in early July and promised American President Bill Clinton that he would do everything to ensure that the intruders pull back. Sitting here, I too get the impression that the war is winding up.

The Kargil operation has been tough on us infantry soldiers. Living in tattered tents and homes vacated by frightened villagers, we continue clearing the peaks. There is so much to be done even after the heights have been recaptured. Just consolidating our hold on these peaks is a huge task because they have been 'registered' by Pakistani artillery, which means they can shell us with extreme accuracy.

First, we had to clear the mines they had strewn all over the approaches to the peaks and on the heights themselves. Casualty evacuation had become difficult and risky because the enemy had also started mining the bodies of our men, also the bunkers they had built, which were too unsafe for us to take shelter in as their openings were facing our positions and they would have to be rebuilt, their direction changed.

The engineers had to be called up to clear the mines – tiny pieces of plastic barely visible to the human eye. They had to also dodge the artillery shells, which still fell with unfailing regularity.

The Pakis had been thrown out of these heights but they were not going to let us rest in peace.

In strategic terms, they had laid out a brilliant plan. But they did not account for the tenacity and raw courage of the Indian soldier. We had fought more than just one enemy on these razor-sharp cliffs and in chilling temperatures. But we finally got them on the run.

They were still holding out on several peaks, but now it was just a matter of time. The evidence of the involvement of the Pakistani Army had been building up and the restraint shown by our side had also given us the diplomatic advantage. That surely must have weighed on the mind of Pakistani Prime Minister Nawaz Sharif when he flew to Washington. We learn, some days later, that before boarding the plane, he had accepted Washington's precondition: that the intruders would have to withdraw and the sanctity of the LoC restored.

We are still cut off from civilization; newspapers are still taking a week to reach us. But we had television sets at base camp and, whenever we were down there, we crowded around to hear the latest news. There is already talk of a ceasefire. This, inevitably, sparked off heated debates among the officers. One side, angered by the loss of men, wants the war to go on. It would give us the chance to kill more Pakistani soldiers now that they seem to be on the run. The other half, more sober and detached, wants the war to end, if only to minimize further loss of human life. At times like these, it is difficult to separate emotion from reason. Officers who lost the most troops in Operation Vijay are the ones most adamant about extending the conflict.

JULY 12

The tide has truly turned. Diplomatically, Pakistan has been humiliated. Militarily, we are in control. On the news, we can see that the reaction in Pakistan to Sharif's Washington visit has grown increasingly hostile. The media and the Opposition parties are castigating him. In the Pakistani press, the families of dead Pakistani soldiers are asking uncomfortable questions. Unlike our soldiers, because of Pakistan's clumsy attempts to deny involvement, their soldiers are not being given a decent burial, leave alone being hailed as martyrs. Many of them still lie on our peaks, flung into valleys and gorges by angry Indian troops. Even after killing the enemy, our troops would go on a rampage, knifing dead bodies.

What were we to do with them? There was no question of taking their bodies down. Pakistan had refused to accept their dead, still keeping the pretence that they were not soldiers but mercenaries. Even our troops were unhappy about having to carry Pakistani bodies down. Carrying our own had been a huge logistical exercise: eight men for one stretcher, so they could take turns and make the seven-to-eight hour journey down the slopes.

On television, we would watch our spokesperson giving a figure for the number of Pakistanis killed. We always wondered how they reached those figures. So many bodies had fallen or been kicked into inaccessible gorges by our men that it was impossible to tell. By now, the fleeing intruders had given up on the exercise of dragging their dead with them. They had to contend with the injured, and that had become their priority. The body of one of their officers had to be brought down by us, mainly for reasons of publicity. The men had slung the body on a donkey and taken him downhill before he was displayed for the cameras. But so many others will probably continue to lie on our side till the snow falls and buries them.

JULY 15

Talk of a withdrawal continues, but on the ground we see no signs of it. We still have to cope with the emotionally draining task of casualty evacuation. Even as late as mid-July, after the DGMOs (Director General Military Operations) of both sides had met to discuss the details of the withdrawal, a shell landed near our *langar* where troops were eating their lunch in the warm afternoon sun. Many were injured and had to be rushed to the Forward Surgical Centre at Gumri.

Our orders are making it clear that the withdrawal of Pakistani troops has been finalized. We are told not to fire at any retreating Pakistani Army regulars. Nothing, it seems, is being left to chance. The Indian government has decided to allow for a smooth withdrawal and ensure there is no resumption of hostilities. Several flag meetings are being held at the unit level, to ensure that Islamabad respects the Washington Declaration signed by Nawaz Sharif on July 4.

Meanwhile, we start preparing for the onset of winter. The enemy may have been defeated, but they have left us a mammoth task. These heights can no longer be left unguarded. We will have to construct shelters, bunkers, arrange food supplies and stocks of ammunition, plus all the other high altitude equipment that has started trickling in. Special shoes, clothing, mountaineering equipment, sleeping bags, night vision equipment. The army inventory will be a large one this year.

SIX

"The war is over"

JULY 16

Is this war really over? After eleven weeks of intense fighting in the most difficult of conditions, and against impossible odds, the mind is still not programmed to relax. Most of us, officers and men, are still mentally on a battle high, where the senses are operating at levels never experienced before: every nerve is stretched, every sound magnified, every sinew alert to the slightest hint of danger. The colonel who had flagged down our convoy at the Sonamarg checkpoint to warn us of the dangers ahead came around distributing sweets. "Congratulations, sir," he said, "the war is over. They have withdrawn. Finally, it's all over. We won."

For the first time in nearly three months, I lie down and stretch my weary legs. Every joint in my body is aching. I want, as do all the others, to sleep for days. But sleep will not come for a long time. This is the legacy Operation Vijay has left us. There will be no more lapses in vigil. Not for the men who will now have to guard these frozen heights. I am to be one of them.

Right now, my mind is filled with thoughts of the dead. There have been so many. Officers whom, just the other day, I played cards with in the mess. The JCOs and other ranks, the jawans who are bonded together as a unit. I try and imagine what Lt Tilak Bannerjee's family must have gone through. He went missing on May 21 and his body was finally found today,

July 16. All those brave soldiers and fellow officers who are now being hailed as the Kargil martyrs. May they rest in peace.

For most of us, the sounds of battle still reverberate in our heads. I find my hand often moving involuntarily to the radio set, to check my weapon, the ammunition. This war will remain with us a long time. I look around at my troops. They, like me, are sprawled out on the ground, faces turned to catch the warmth of the sun. Even reclining, their bodies are tense, their eyes alert. They have learnt to be careful, to sit behind a boulder, expecting the shells to still come screaming in. Just that morning, Major-General Mohinder Puri had come around to each unit with words of caution. "Expect anything from them. They will be thirsting for revenge. Treat them like you would treat a wounded animal," he had said.

We know that only too well. Suddenly, after a gap of 27 years, the Siachen Glacier – the highest battlefield – has extended itself to include an additional 150 km of the Kargil sector. There can no longer be any complacency. Nor time for a bit of rest and recuperation. Preparations have to be made to hold the heights through winter and that entails a huge task. We now have to sit on these peaks all through the year, come winter, summer, rain or snow. The question in all our minds, obviously, is: If we can do it now, why did we abandon them for the last so many years?

JULY 27

The price for ignoring the Kargil sector as a possible avenue of intrusion is being paid now. We are eyeball to eyeball with their regular troops all along this newly created theatre of tension. The Government of India and the Ministry of Defence will never admit to this, but even now, ten days after the war is officially 'over', some Pakistani intruders still occupy some points on our side of the border. Strategically, it does not offer them much advantage. But the fact remains that in Drass, opposite Point 5100, on a feature called Saddle, the Pakistanis are at least 800 yards into our territory and we can do little about it. Much later, a plan to evict them is drawn up, but the government is not keen.

Ten days after the withdrawal was touted as being complete on July 17, the Pakistani Army heli-dropped its troops close to this feature and opened up with their artillery guns. 16 Grenadiers were there, in the process of firming up their hold on other vacated peaks at Saddle, when suddenly the shells started landing. They weren't really prepared. The withdrawal had been completed and formalized and the Grenadiers were taken by surprise. Caught in the open, the troops started running downhill, the shells chasing them as they scrambled down the slopes.

Total pandemonium had broken out. Why were the Pakis firing again? Was the war not over? That was one of the most tension-filled days of the entire battle for Brigadier Aul. Despite several attempts, he could not get through on radio to any officer. He did, initially, manage to speak to Captain Uday but he was hit by a shell and had to be evacuated (a feature on Saddle is now known as Uday Hill). All that Brigade Headquarters knew was that a sudden attack had been launched, violating the ceasefire. Aul wanted more details, but there was no contact. All he knew was that there were several casualties.

All night, Aul had sat in his office at Brigade Headquarters trying to find out what was happening. It was much later that Brigade learnt the truth: that the Pakistanis were still occupying Indian territory, and still are. Plans for dislodging them were drawn up but for some inexplicable reason, they were called off. Maybe because such a move was fraught with political danger. What if that sparked off the battle once again? It was perhaps a risk the caretaker government didn't want to take, not with elections round the corner. Fortunately for the government, the media had emptied out of the sector and the incident went completely unreported.

JULY 31

For us, the incident just brought home a lesson we had already learnt: there is no room for complacency. The commanders who had dismissed Brigadier Sumanwar's presentation during the war games in April had made fools of themselves, but now we have been left to pay the price. And what a price! There is no taste of victory, no time to celebrate or for the men to spend time with their families, even though many came so close to death. We will still spend our days in snow that rises to twenty and thirty feet. We feel like anything but heroes. It is still a question of life and death.

Proof of occupation. Pakistani army regulars who settled in Indian territory as early as January 26, 1999 and engraved their names on a height in Drass.

Bofors guns deployed in the war theatre in Kargil.

Indian soldiers with Bofors guns waiting for orders to fire during the Kargil War.

Indian soldiers fire artillery in the Kargil sector against a Pakistani-backed armed intrusion.

Stretcher bearers bringing a dead comrade back; one of many who was devoured by the mountains.

An injured soldier being brought back from the mountains of death.

Indian soldiers taking artillery equipment up the mountains.

Helicopter sorties flew back and forth bringing casualties to the makeshift hospital.

Soldiers celebrate the success of Operation Vijay.

An officer breaks down after the capture of Tololing. The feature had been cleared but he had lost too many men.

Pakistani bodies being given a burial.

A moment of triumph. Soldiers hoist the Indian tricolour to re-establish their hold over a peak in Mushkoh.

Captain Jayashree salutes the body of her husband, Major Vivek Gupta, of 2nd Rajputana Rifles who lost his life fighting in the battle for Tololing.

The Indian army and the air force lost 474 men, while as many as 1109 were wounded.

SEPTEMBER 28

We try to equip ourselves as well as we can but already we are having to deal with more bodies of soldiers dying of high altitude pulmonary oedema (HAPO). Some others are being treated for frostbite. In this intense cold, taking off your gloves for a minute, necessary to obey calls of nature, is an invitation to frostbite.

The men are exhausted from erecting the new bunkers, made of fibre-reinforced plastic. But first, the men have to go out to clear the snow. We have already had the first snowfall in the higher reaches. It has to be beaten down so the tracks don't disappear. This is an avalanche-prone area and the bunkers have to be strategically located. Obviously, not every inch of the LoC can be guarded by foot soldiers. There are gaps between bunkers and for a patrol party to walk through the snow and cover a distance of only one kilometer takes between five and seven hours.

That is mostly what we are doing now, to protect the peaks. Teaching our boys the use of mountaineering equipment and snowmobiles. Teaching them to survive on meagre rations, in case the weather does not permit supplies to reach us at the forward posts. To subsist on what we call Compo Ration, which comprises 125 grams of vegetable pulao, 100 grams of *suji halwa* and some tea bags. There is also an emergency survival kit comprising a chocolate bar and some *chikki,* which is manufactured in Hyderabad and packed by the Defence Food Research Laboratory in Mysore.

If you fall sick, you have to pray that the hepter (helicopter) can land through the clouds which envelop us ever so often. HAPO bags and emergency medical kits have been kept in all the posts but they don't always suffice. Every unit has only one doctor each and he can't possibly be in all the posts or even handy when needed. There are nursing assistants too but then there is little that they can do when your body gives up after being perpetually exposed to freezing winds, blizzards and avalanches.

Even when the hepters come in to land, the men have to furiously beat the snow and unroll the fibre-reinforced plastic so the chopper can make its descent. The only time I see some semblance of a smile on the faces of the men is when the mailbag arrives. It is the only thing that gives them warmth – those letters from home which bring them news of their families, their children and their parents.

OCTOBER 15

Guard duty is the worst possible assignment. All night, the men have to sit in the freezing cold, eyes glued to the night vision devices which we have belatedly been issued. The army has been doing some hasty shopping. Apart from the NVDs, we now have decent Extremely Cold Climate Uniforms and proper alpine snow boots. It's on these peaks, at heights ranging between 12,000 and 18,000 feet, that we have now made our homes. The posts and structures had to be in place and equipped before the snow started. So everything has to be carried up by mules or airlifted – food, kerosene oil, medicines, arms and ammunition.

OCTOBER 18

Every day is a nightmare; brigade commanders total up the number of sorties made by the Mi-17s carrying supplies. Every evening, a report is submitted to Maj Gen Puri, who in turn informs Corps of the progress. Maj Gen Puri is in charge of the entire sector from Kaobal Gali in Kupwara at one end to Chorbat La at the other. Mules make their way up tracks, as far as they can go, after which supplies have to be carried by the troops. This exercise will carry on through October. So many helipads have to be constructed for airlifting supplies. Just carrying the fibre-reinforced plastic sheets is a task that seems to take forever. Each hut that houses four to six men weighs around 1500 kg. Each Mi-17 carries a load of about 1000 kg. So, three sorties have to be made for every two huts.

In terms of rations, each man requires 1.7 kg of food and 2.7 litres of kerosene oil per day. Add to this the 500 g of special rations comprising soup packets, dry fruit and Frooti tetrapacks, which constitute high-nutrition food. For approximately 200 days of winter, it is necessary to stock one tonne per person and there are at least 20,000 troops now committed to holding the heights. And these don't include men drawn from support battalions like supply, ordnance and medical etc.

There is a new Forward Surgical Centre which has come up at Drass now. An internally-heated underground hospital, which from experience is considered necessary in this sector. One thing is certain: the winter will take its own toll, and irrespective of the FiAPO and FLACO bags that have been provided for in the forward posts, the doctors will continue to struggle to save frostbitten toes and fingers.

It is a no-war, no-peace situation. Artillery guns are in battle-ready mode and we are on constant alert. In this sector, far more treacherous than Siachen where there are roads that take you at least up to base camp, the approaches go through deep gorges. It is these gorges and peaks that an entire division of the army is now going to protect, unlike earlier when a brigade was in charge. During the war itself, five additional brigades had to be brought in to rescue Indian territory.

Territory is now being measured in terms of financial cost. Siachen they say costs an approximate four crore a day, Kargil will need at least ten crore a day. It's worth it, they'll tell you, to defend the nation's honour. And as they keep telling us: always be on guard, Pakistan now has a military executive heading their country. The same General Pervez Musharraf who conceived of the Kargil intrusion.

We did our bit. We went beyond the call of duty. We fought in frozen wastelands where the snow often turned red. We struggled with faulty weapons but we did not turn back. We climbed dizzy heights, sometimes only to bring back our dead. But, we continued. We will continue to guard our borders and suffer the vagaries of weather. There is just about enough space for our men to sit in these snow habitats; lying down is a luxury, but they will continue uncomplainingly. This is, after all, the Indian Army. And we are, after all, doing our duty. It has to be done because, even though we forced the intruders out, we really didn't win the war. If we had, we wouldn't be sitting here – eyeball to eyeball.

SEVEN

"Intelligence is an important factor in operations... the present set up is not designed for this"

In one sense, the Kargil operation was a plus. Not in terms of the victory, but because of the crucial lessons that came out of it. Army Headquarters and the defence ministry realized just how ill-prepared we were and just how vulnerable the lack of proper equipment left us. In terms of proper equipment, the lesson has clearly been learnt. Over the last three months, adequate high altitude equipment and clothing have started flowing in, making life a little easier for the officers and men who now have to guard a new stretch of inhospitable border.

But there were other lessons that were as, if not more, crucial, relating to the total lack of intelligence gathering. Some advanced intelligence gathering equipment like electronic sensors, radars and night vision devices have been ordered and will arrive, but the main problem we faced was with human intelligence. The various intelligence agencies responsible, from RAW to Military Intelligence, failed in their primary job: to alert the country to an intrusion by hundreds of enemy soldiers. It was an intelligence failure of Himalayan proportions and a number of brave men paid for the lapse with their lives.

This is clearly the most crucial lesson of the war: that we had fought a critical, difficult battle in an information void. There was little if any intelligence even halfway through the battle. 14 JAK Rifles were told they were up against 'a handful of mercenaries'. They counted 240 regular army soldiers walking back across the LoC at Kaksar once the withdrawal was announced. Such disinformation caused untold damage. If we did not know the numbers, and were always underestimating, this meant we were also constantly underestimating their weapon-holding capabilities. We officers all agree on the need to upgrade our electronic surveillance. In retrospect, now that the battle is officially over, we also realize the lack of a proper joint intelligence apparatus at the national level.

Officers at Northern Command tell me that there is hardly any coordination between the plethora of different agencies: Military Intelligence, Intelligence Bureau (IB) and RAW, all of which are active in Kashmir. While RAW had failed to give any information pertaining to the buildup at the border; IB had passed on information, which is now being pushed under the carpet. As early as June 2, its director, Shyamal Dutta, had penned his signature to a note, which went right up to the prime minister and our DGMO, regarding a build up in the sector. It had also talked of increased helicopter activity at Skardu, but our officers in Delhi now say that IB has a habit of sending such notes all the time.

Moreover, there is so much distrust between the agencies. IB's staff in Kashmir reports to its head office in Delhi. Seldom, as we officers in CI Ops will confirm, is this information shared at the local level. The distrust is evident in the meetings of the Unified Headquarters in Srinagar. There were, according to officers present, constant arguments and differences in perception. IB and RAW are already accusing 15 Corps of underplaying the number of militants and mercenaries who infiltrated the state. Finally, Corps decided to put on record the various intelligence inputs from all the agencies.

An exercise unearths the fact that the note that Shyamal Dutta sent on June 2 stayed at the DGMO's office. The information was not even communicated to Northern Command or to the Joint Intelligence Committee. The explanation given later: IB notes are very general in nature and basically an attempt to cover up for any failures. Hence, all their notes invariably mention that infiltration is expected from Kargil and Rajouri and Poonch and Uri and Kupwara.

Commanders of all units have listed the lack of information as one of the major drawbacks of Operation Vijay. Brigadier Aul states quite categorically in his report that the initial intrusion in the Drass sector was noticed by 16 Grenadiers only on May 8. When the Brigade was shifted rapidly from the counter-insurgency grid to conventional operations, the information regarding the enemy strength and disposition was vague. Then, the intrusion was not even considered a serious matter and it was felt that the intruders could be evicted with ease.

The report submitted by 56 Brigade is emphatic. It says: "In view of the failure of various intelligence agencies to detect the intrusion till as late as May, there was a total vacuum as far as operational intelligence was concerned. The initial misdirection and slow progress of operations can be attributed to the scarce intelligence available about the enemy disposition and their state of preparedness. The holding formation (16 Grenadiers) could also not provide much intelligence about the terrain conditions and layout of features held by the enemy. For operations launched in the initial stages, no time was given for recce, planning and preparation. This was possibly due to incorrect intelligence assessment and pressures to evict the intruders as soon as possible. This resulted in low confidence of battalion commanders and company commanders in achieving the objectives assigned to them and therefore very little could be achieved in the initial stages... The units were not aware of the areas under shelling while moving into the sector."

The report continues: "Information of terrain in Mushkoh and Drass was vague... Intelligence is an important factor in operations. To maintain surveillance over a large frontage in inhospitable and difficult mountainous terrain and to fight a successful defensive/offensive battle in high altitude area, there is a need to gain constant information about the enemy and the terrain in the area of operations. A plethora of sources that have now become available provide a large amount of information, which needs to be analyzed in detail. Staff should be capable of collecting, collating and interpreting information and disseminating it to the troops in a near-real-time frame. The present set-up is not designed for this and requires being reorganized for sources indicated below:

Specialist troops trained to operate in glaciated/high altitude terrain with specialist equipment/vehicles for gathering information should form an integral part of the formation. There would also be a need to equip these troops with snowmobiles. It is preferable to integrate local scout battalions having an intimate knowledge of the terrain with the formations.

Electronic surveillance: suitable electronic surveillance means like unattended sensors and radars with day and night surveillance capabilities should be introduced to identify concentration/movement of troops and gun positions.

Satellite pictures of high resolution and aerial photographs should supplement intelligence gathering to facilitate sound planning at the formation/unit level.

Electronic intelligence resources are presently centralized at the Corps level. These must be decentralized to the Division level.

The enemy had catered for air defence capability in the form of 12.7 mm guns and stinger missiles. This degraded air strikes and movement of our own hepters close to enemy defences to quite an extent. Troops must therefore be provided with air defence capabilities. SAMs and Twin Barrel AD guns will greatly enhance the limited air defence capability of an infantry battalion.

For movement of tactical loads and heavy guns and ammunition to forward posts, hepters should be made available.

Another lesson, which our commanders must never forget, is that it is no longer enough to just train for counter-insurgency operations. We had all been cast in that mould and had great difficulty in switching to conventional warfare. What 14 JAK Rif's report says holds good for each one of us: "Adequate time should be given for conventional training of troops in CI Ops. The mere statement that training should be conducted while on CI duties, does not suffice."

The preponderance of artillery fire and the use of Bofors in the direct fire role proved to be a battle-winning factor. Direct firing of Bofors paid heavy dividends in terms of unsettling the enemy as well as raising the morale of our own troops.

Our success in various operations is attributable to our junior leaders. It is essential to maintain a very high quality of training.

Adequate special clothing and mountaineering equipment was not available but grit and determination enabled the troops to brave subzeroes.

Feint attacks divided the enemy attention and prevented him from sending reinforcements to threatened areas.

If any confirmation was needed of the abysmal intelligence failure, it has now been provided by the report of the Kargil Review Committee chaired by K. Subrahmanyam. Placed in Parliament, the report details the critical failure in intelligence. None of the agencies involved, particularly the RAW, provided the slightest warning of possible intrusions.

The report also confirms that the intrusions took place much earlier than the army brass was willing to admit at the time. The report states: "Reconnaissance parties comprising officers started crossing the LoC in late January/early February. They established a first line of administrative bases within a limited distance across the LoC in February... Care was exercised by the intruders to move only in the gaps between the Indian winter posts and to avoid detection by Winter Air Surveillance Operations (WASO)... WASO helicopters and operational reconnaissance flights repeatedly flew over them as is evident from one of the diaries captured in Mushkoh Valley. A combination of factors prevented their detection: camouflage clothing; helicopter vibrations which hampered observation, opportunity for concealment on hearing the sound of approaching helicopters, and peace time safety requirements of maintaining a certain height above the ground and a given distance from the LoC. Since the effort was largely to detect infiltration, most flights flew along valleys and not across the ridges. All these factors made the WASO patrols of negligible value."

The report has been highly critical of all the intelligence-gathering agencies and recommended an overhaul of the entire system. The government has accepted the suggestion, but whether the required changes and intelligence overhaul will happen on the ground is debatable. Without a drastic improvement in coordination and proper surveillance equipment, the kind of operational failures that I have detailed through the pages of this diary will continue to take place.

In fact, the operational failures which cost so many lives were not even within the ambit of the Kargil Review Committee. With the Pakistan Army continuing to infiltrate across the border and the loss of additional soldiers to such attacks, the issue of operational failure acquires added urgency.

Maybe this diary will expose those responsible. But who will pay the price? My overwhelming fear is that the sacrifices of so many brave soldiers will have been in vain…

ANNEXURES

Annexure A

Extracts from the personal diary of Lt Muhammad Maaz Ullah Khan, 8 Northern Light Infantry, Pakistan Army, recovered from Point 4812.

Jan 1: Happy new year. Started off from Rawalpindi at 1400 hours for Skardu by bus, after repeated fruitless tries at the Islamabad international (airport). At Iftaar, we were at Mansehra, so called home from there. At 2200 hours we were at Beshaw, called home again.

Jan 2: Reached Skardu at 1000 hrs and reported to the unit (8NLI). Capt Mueed Shams Khan was Adjt (Adjutant) Also Capt Shehryar, Capt Imran and Capt Sarfraz are there. Major Raheem and Maj Qazi were CO and 2iC respectively. Nice team of officers.

Jan 13: 1st day at Baltoro sector. Today, I along with Capt Dr Salah-ud-din Masood got inducted in Baltoro sector. We moved on a jeep and a pick-up. Reached Dassu at 1530 hrs. Left Dassu for Apoligin at 1600 hrs and at Iftar time, we reached Apoligin. We sent the vehicles back and stayed the night there.

Jan 27: We left Shama for IHEC. Another tough leg. Reached IHEC at 1630 hrs. Received by Maj Amjad (2iC 38 Mtn Arty) Maj Tariq Mehmood (Zulu), Capt Sarwar and Lt Aamer ex 38 Mtn Arty. Disappointed to find TV and V-SAT out of order.

Jan 31: Heli msn (Helicopter mission) came consisting of 2xLama's and lx Mi-17 TV set sent for repair. Bundles of eatable and mail were received. I got 1 Eid Card from Aapa, 1 letter/Eid card from Asif, lx ltrs from Mussarrat Abbas, 1x card from Capt Naveed and 1 diary (this one) from Tariq Mamoo.

Feb 1: 6th day at IHEC. I took a bath. Terrible experience – taking a bath at 19,000 ft, at – 22 degrees centigrade. Capt Dr Salah-ud-din Masood left for Nawaz camp on his way to Conwoy Saddle. I will be moving up along Capt Sarwar on 10 Feb.

Feb 3: It is my 8th day at IHEC. I felt like going for a walk, so made a round trip of the camp, helipad and Gun position. I got an idea of firing the 12.7 mm HMG. Got permission from Zulu and tested the fire of HMG. Nice experience!

Feb 4: It is my 9th day at IHEC. The day is crystal clear and sunny. Zulu decided to check the guns. So the clear sunny day was celebrated in the roars and thunders of 105 mm Mtn Guns.

Last night, sky was all clear with stars and moon shining overhead. It was a beautiful scene as the snow-covered peaks were glistening in moonlight. I sat alone outside at midnight. It made me recall the time when I and Saloo used to sit on rooftop of our block at Quetta and talk whole night on a pack of cigarette. Good days!

Feb 5: 10th day at IHEC. Another clear day although not sunny. Saddle all visible with its igloos appearing like black dots on white surface. Last night, again the sky was crystal again. Temp falling, at -30 degree C, as I checked the thermometer in the morning. Today, Heli -msn again didn't come despite some clear weather.

Feb 10: 15th day at IHEC. After spending two weeks at IHEC today, we left for Nawaz Camp on our way to Conwoy Saddle – the final frontier. Started at 1530 hours, we reached at 1700 hrs. Capt Sarwar, ex 38 Mtn is accompanying me.

Feb 11: 30th day in Baltoro sector. We left from Nawaz Camp at 0800 hrs in bad weather but by the grace of Allah, it cleared after we crossed C-5 (Rel Pt). Reached the Saddle Camp at 1500 hrs. Capt Dr Salah-ud-din received us with SMG fire.

Feb 12: 2nd day at Saddle. Whole night it snowed heavily and the igloo was choked in the morning. I dug through the snow and crawled out of the igloo. Whole day, I, Capt Sarwar, and Capt Dr Salah-ud-din kept on digging the igloo out. Today, despite clear weather, Heli msn didn't come due to bad weather at G-l.

Feb 13: *Ahmad Faraz said,* En barishon se dosti achhi nahi Faraz, kuchha makaan hai, kuchh to khayal karo..."

Feb 15: 5th day at Saddle. After breakfast, I, Himmat Wali and Sayed Alam worked on the officer's igloo in snowy wind and dug out a good way into the igloo. At least after this much hard work, Allah will have mercy and the igloo will not be checked tonight. Today, Himmat Wali and party could not go down even after completing their 21-day tenure, due to adverse weather.

Feb 16: 6th day at Saddle. Again, Himmat Wali and party couldn't be relieved due to bad weather.

Feb 17: 7th day at Saddle. Weather is clear today. Mi-17 made special emergency msn for kerosene oil supply at Saddle, but due to some low clouds and snowy wind it couldn't come beyond Nawaz Camp despite three attempts between 1200 & 1630 hrs. We were very enthusiastic but later became disappointed.

Feb 19: 9th day at Saddle. Normal weather with snowy wind in early morning. Later the wind stopped and light snow shower started. At sunset, the weather got clearer and we could see the moon and stars through thin high clouds. At about 2000, the clouds vanished and a clear sky with shining stars appeared although the moon went down. Zulu informed us at 2100 that tomorrow in case of clear weather, the Heli msn will arrive, *Insha Allah.*

Feb 20: Weather was clear today, although not sunny. Heli reportedly went to Shakma so no chance. We went to Fwd Saddle. I took along Styre Snipes and shot at Indian Posn (position).

Feb 21: A very clear and sunny day. I enjoyed the beautiful sunrise on snowy peaks. Did some nice photography. Heli msn came at 1130. Mi-17 dropped a sling which contained my personal demand as well as ration supplies and K-ii oil. So we had a nice dinner with chicken, Pepsi and egg pudding. Again a clear night today. Weather is getting nice.

Feb 24: Early morning we were given Alert by Zarrar HQ regarding Hel Borne Op. I got the two 12.7 and the 14.5 ready with ammo. Tested SMG for zeroing. Now let the en (enemy) come. Capt Dr Sohail is today at Nawaz on his way to relieve Capt Dr Salah-ud-din. Will be here tomorrow. I am expecting 15 ltrs (letters). Let's see who all wrote them.

Feb 25: Capt Dr Sohail Aslam arrived with his party. The party brought me 15 letters and sweets and Pepsi tins from Zulu. Sweets from Nirala was a good addition. I received 7 letters from Abbu/Ammi, two from Aapa/Obaid Bhai, a card from Salman and OER extracts from unit and some cards from course mates. I was happy to find that Salman has got the scholarship from France for MBA. It is all his talent and Allah's blessing.

Feb 26: Whole day it was sunny and I enjoyed the sun by offering the three prayers (*Zohr, Asr, Maghrib*) outside. The night is also clear with moon and stars shining overhead.

Feb 27: Another crystal clear day. Allah is very kind to his soldiers. I got the magazine opened and enjoyed the fire of 60 mm mortar. I fired three rounds myself. No Heli msn. Night is also clear with moon and stars.

Feb 28: 18th day at Saddle. Another crystal clear, sunny day. Today, the Heli-msn were conducted. Dr Sohail got his demand – Pepsi, Bread, Nimke, Dry Fruit etc. Mi-17 was in good hands. Good droppings. Other than ration, K II, we got fresh fruit as well – oranges. Zulu had asked Capt Murtaza at Paiju to send Malta at Saddle. Just imagine!

March 1: Although the ni clear and full of stars, the morning got cloudy, yet clear and pleasant. I tested HE 36 hand grenades – two of them. It was a lot of 1963. So, as expected, they didn't go off. Still the Blinds are lying on South-Western slope about 50 yards from the camp down below. No danger.

March 2: Again, wind and snow but not that bad. Hopingly, it will be clear tomorrow morning for us to go down. Oh yes! we are completing 21 days at Saddle tomorrow and getting down also. Got my luggage packed and fasted the krympons to my shoes. All set to go, by Allah Almighty's grace.

March 3: We couldn't get down due to bad weather. Now another day is there at Saddle. Let's see.

March 4: Today finally we got down from Saddle. Capt Aftab and Capt Tariq relieved myself and Captain Sarwar respectively. Although not very clear weather, but we moved anyway. Got down to IHEC and received by Maj Tariq (Zulu) and Co. What a change. Television is operational along with the Dish. But unfortunately, telephone is out of order.

March 5: 52nd day at Baltoro. Still, I am at IHEC. Tomorrow, I have to move to Shama on my way to Paiju to relieve Capt Murtaza. At Paiju, I'll have to stay for at least 25 days.

March 6: Bad weather didn't allow us to move. Continual blizzard with snowfall made it impossible. We saw the PTV awards ceremony at night.

March 7: Again we couldn't move due to Blizzard and bad weather. Instead, we saw *"Doli Saja Ke Rakhna"* on Zee TV at ni.

March 8: 55th day in Baltoro sector and 5th day at IHEC. Again, couldn't move due to bad weather. Let's see what happens tomorrow.

March 9: A nice and clear morning and so I left for Shama at 0900 although I couldn't see other officers as they were sleeping. At about 1100, when we were about to come out of the Nullah, two Lamas flew overhead to IHEC. They took the cas and our Zulu Maj Tariq back to Skardu. So Maj Tariq is also relieved today by Maj Khurshid. We reached Shama at 1600 hrs. A tough walk as there was lot of snow and lot of weight on me.

March 10: Left Shama for Concordia. A clear day but due to a lot of snow, a difficult move. Actually, we are the first party after recent snowfall, so we are doing track-beating.

March 11: Left Concordia for Gora II. Met Dr Javed on the way. Reached Gora II around 1300 hrs. Decided to go ahead up to Gora I. So moved on and replaced Gora I at 1700 hrs. Received by Dr Wasif, Capt Faisal, Capt Mudassar.

March 12: Stayed at Gora-I and had a rest. Talked home through wrls (wireless).

March 13: Left Gora I for Urdukas. Reached there at 1045 hrs and after tea moved on to Paiju at 1200 hrs. Reached

Paiju at 1730 hrs. Here, I'll stay for a month as today is my 60th day in Baltoro.

March 14: Inspected the containers of K-2 dropped by C-13-yesterday. Arranged their dumping and had a recce for hunting. It's a hunter's Paradise.

March 15: Kept on roaming in the area for a hunt but no success. In the evening, Capt Sarwar came with his party from Urdukas. I have got some company at least. Sep Mubarak Ali is with the party. I have told him to take my letters to Mianwali on his way home. So I am writing a detailed letter to Abbu and Ammi. Got three bottles of Pepsi from Capt Aftab's pack. These were sent for us by Capt Nabi Baksh. Also got a radio and a pack of cards from Capt Aftab.

March 16: Again no success in hunting. At sunset, Capt Dr Wasif reached here direct from Gora-I. So I have got a good company now. Weather is getting worse as strong wind is blowing.

March 17: I got a success and hunted a duck but a small one. Weather is still the same. Wind is getting stronger.

March 18: 65th day at Baltoro. Capt Sarwar and Capt Dr Wasif along with their party moved down to Askoli direct. I am again alone at Paiju. I have given four letters to Sep Mubarak Ali for Ammi and Abbu and four letters to Dr Wasif for Salman, Salman Arshad and Obaid Bhai.

March 19: Kept resting all day. Weather still not clear. Sudedar Maqsood scored a duck today.

March 20: Kept resting. At noon, went up the mountain for a recce but couldn't find enough way due to snow. Today, weather was crystal clear but no Heli -msn was conducted.

March 21: Nothing special. Weather is again windy and cloudy.

March 22: No special activity. Kept resting and listening to the radio.

March 23: Pakistan Day is being observed all over the country. I listened to the Pak Day Parade and President's address on Radio. We'll be wearing another medal now, so I have got a total of five medals now – Quite Senior.

March 24: Strong wind is blowing outside although the night was clear. A good news – our unit (8 NLI) is not going to Peyun, instead it is heard that we were moving to Punjab. I wish and pray that we move to Lahore. NLI has been made a Regular Infantry Regiment. I plan to get myself posted permanently to 8 NLI as a parental officer. Allah make it good for me.

March 25: Still weather is worse. No activity during day. At night, Adjutant Nabi Bukhsh called on wrls. Major Raheem was also on the set. We had a good chat. Heli-msn and C-130 droppings are planned tomorrow. So far, weather is getting better and the night is clear.

March 26: The morning was not clear but around 1000 hrs, the clouds vanished. We got the report that C-130 was taking off from Rwp (Rawalpindi) at 1100 hrs but it went back from the way as the clouds again covered the sky over Baltoro and snowfall started. So, we sat back disappointed. Anyhow, in the evening, weather again got clear. We pray that it remain clear tomorrow so we may get some ration and aid for Eid.

March 27: Day was absolutely clear and sunny. Heli msn was planned and we kept waiting but to our disappointment, Heli didn't appear.

March 28: Day was absolutely clear and at about 1000 hrs, heli appeared. Co was also along. We got the ration and some demands and letters. I received two letters from Asif, one from home, one from Capt Z.A. Sulehri. Plus, I received my cassette player and cassettes. We sent slings and packs of ration to Saddle and other posts. Capt Adnan and Capt Dr Tariq also arrived at noon from P-II.

March 29: EID MUBARAK! I, Capt Adnan, and Dr Sahib are here at Paiju. Although it's Eid day but there's nothing special. Again weather has gone worst. Very low clouds, snowfall and strong wind is there. So we remained restricted to our room. Kept listening to music and smoking. I received sig msg (signal message) that Capt Nabi Bukhsh has called my home and my parents have received my letters and Eid greetings that I sent by Sp Mubarik Ali. OB, Aapa and Salman are also at Mianwali. My 3rd Eid out of home and away from my parents.

March 30: Capt Adnan and Dr Sahib have departed for Urdukas. I along with Fida went to Pari II and saw the LoC for building another barrack there. Selected and marked the LoC and came back. On the way back, I scored a duck. A tiring walk – four hrs one way.

March 31: Weather has gone adverse. Low clouds down to earth and snowfall with strong wind. Kept listening to music – *Dil Se* and *Kuch Kuch Hota Hai* – badly missed SAC. I have got a nice attachment with this music as we had a very memorable time together at Quetta and this was the official music of our course. Happy memories!

April 1: 79th day at Baltoro and 20th day at Paiju. It's the first of April and no one here to fool with. Weather is getting worst. Snowfall with strong wind. No chance of any outing so kept on listening to the music and smoking and dreaming of good days. My stock of coffee is also no more. So just passing time.

April 2: Still weather is adverse. Snowfall and strong wind is on. All activities ceased. My stock of cigarettes is coming to an end and there is no chance of Heli -msn in near future. So just passing time somehow.

April 3: 81st day at Baltoro. Weather has suddenly cleared and Heli -msn is awaited. Good for us. I got my demand. Casualties awaited.

April 4: Weather is clear and CO is here at 0800 hrs with Mi-17. GOC is awaited. I have received a parcel from home carrying sweets. GOC arrived at 1100 hrs and after talking to the tps (troops), visited IHEC as well.

April 5: Weather is again trying to go worse. But till noon it is still high clouds. Afternoon – unexpectedly Heli-msn has arrived. But due to low clouds at Gora-I and onwards, it went back. I gave Maj Shahid a letter for SAC and Tel msg for Salman as he is going to Rwp. Let's hope he doesn't forget.

April 6: 84th day at Baltoro and 25th day at Paiju. Weather is clear and pleasant. No special activity. Kept resting.

April 7: Sky is again covered with clouds. RE of sub Maqsood is here. N/sub Niat Wali is taking over charge. Also CQMH Hadi is here and taking over charge from Mumtaz. No other certain activity.

April 8: Heavy snowfall with windstorm has ceased all movement.

April 9: My 90 days' tenure at Baltoro is coming to an end but it seems that I'll have to overstay my tenure as Capt Mudasar has been evacuated and Capt Aftab has been made to climb the Saddle again. Now Capt Adnan will relieve Capt Aftab and in turn he'll come down and relieve me. Let's see when?

April 10: Weather not clear. Snowfall and wind is on. No certain activity.

April 11: Around 1500 hrs, an avalanche came from the top behind offrs accommodation, although it stopped short of my room but the wind storm it brought along took the roof off the building. Thanks Allah, no harm has been done.

April 12: At 0200 hrs, avalanche again struck Paiju post, this time of higher intensity. Again the roof of barrack went off which we had repaired during day. Let's hope and pray that rest of the night goes well. All day, clouds kept covering the sky and wind kept blowing at a fast pace. Sub Maqsood and Fida went off today to Pari-II on their way to Dassu. I gave Fida 4xltrs for home, O.B., Salman and Asif. He'll be out of sector by 15 or 16 April.

April 13: 91st day at Baltoro and 32nd day at Paiju. Duststorm is on and all activities ceased.

April 14: A relatively clear day with high clouds and no wind. Anwar Shah and party brought some meat of Markhoor from the mountains. This one was hunted some days back and meat was stored in a cave under the snow. A delicious dinner is awaited.

April 15: A clear and sunny day. Heli -msn came and so did Maj Ali Ijaz (2iC, 8NLI). Thanks Allah, CO is not here. My demand for cigarettes has come. Coffee is available now. Maj Anwar and Capt Babar are with the Heli and are served with coffee. Capt Aftab has got down from Saddle today and is at IHEC.

April 16: Again a clear and sunny day. I am waiting for Capt Aftab to reach Paiju and relieve me. Anwar Shah scored a Ram Chakoor today. So a delicious dinner is expected.

April 17: 95th day at Baltoro. Another clear day. We enjoyed the sun. Maj Aftab is still at IHEC. My stock of cigarettes is coming to an end now.

April 18: Weather is again cloudy and windy. Capt Aftab is still at IHEC and it is my 37th day at Paiju.

April 20: Two Lamas came on emergency basis for cas evac from IHEC. Capt Aftab also came with it, so finally my rel is here and I am now preparing for my de-induction.

April 21: Due to adverse weather, I am still at Paiju. Move was not possible. Now I am planning about tomorrow if weather permits.

April 22: 100th day at Baltoro. Still weather is not getting clear.

April 23: Started off from Paiju at 0645 hrs and reached P-II at 1000 hrs. On the way, I met Capt Salman (8 NLI, ex 30 FF) and Capt D.R. Nasir who were moving from P-II to Paiju on their upward move. I had tea at P-II and left for P-I at 1030. Had lunch at P-I and left for Askdi. Reached Askdi at 1700 hrs. Stayed the ni.

April 24: Left Askdi for Apoligon at 0800 hrs. Reached Apoligon at 1500 hrs and had lunch there. At 1800 hrs, Maj Ateeq (New Zulu) came with his party on Toyota pickup. On the same veh (vehicle), I moved down and reached Dassu base campt at 1900 hrs. Stayed the ni.

April 25: 103rd day at Baltoro. I got de-inducted from Baltoro sector and reached Skardu around 1100 hrs. Called home from mess and talked to Ammi, Abbu and Salman. Got my haircut done and shaved. I am back to civilization.

April 26: Whole day, I kept resting and had a good sleep of about 18 hours. At ni, again, called home and spoke to Obaid Bhai and Aapa. Salman is also at Lahore. Maj Ahmed Khan Jiwana (7 NLI, ex 9 FF) is also here at Skardu, he called Lahore to Saif Bhai and I also talked to him. Tomorrow, it is again a holiday Next working day is 28th and the same very day, I'll try to go through the interviews of CO and Brigade Commander, so the next day, on 29th, I may move to Rawalpindi/Islamabad on leave. I'll try to get P/ leave (Privelege leave). Let's see.

April 30: Today at 0700 hrs, I alongwith Maj Arshad left for Islamabad by air. I have got 20 days leave from 1 to 20 May.

June 4: COAS visit expected today to Hamzigond Due to shelling and weather, COAS couldn't come ahead. He only visited Shakma, Gultari and Siachen. AT 1430, I and CO moved to Skardu for weekend.

June 7: I am moving back from Skardu to Hamzigond after spending the weekend. In the morning, I received a parcel from home carrying sweets, toffees, chewing gum, chocolates, etc. plus a Birthday card.

June 12: My 27th birthday. At Hamzigond, Maj Tariq and Nabi Bukhsh are accompanying me. We enjoyed the sweets from home. A bad news. Comd 62 Bde, Brig Nusrat Sial embraced shahadat in Heli crash.

June 13: Today, I am going to be inducted in Tanvir sector. At 1945 hrs, I moved to Ganokh on wheels and stayed the night there. Capt Asim, Capt Mudassar, Lt Khalid and Lt Imran, ex 5 NLI and Lt Shoeb, ex 101 engrs (engineers) were also there.

June 14: 2nd day in the sector. I stayed at Ganokh for acclimatisation.

June 15: 3rd day and I moved to Imtiaz with my party. Moved further on and reached Riaz Base to relieve Capt Qammar. Capt Qammar had captured Flight Lieutenant Nachiketa of IAF. He showed me Nachi's eqpt and the wreckage of the plane. We photographed as well.

June 16: Let's go to war. Early morning, Capt Qammar moved down to Imtiaz. At 1100 hrs, I got a call from Saddle that Badar has been bombarded and destroyed by Indian aircraft. Maj Jawad (5NLI), Maj Ali (CS), Maj Zikriya (ISI), Capt Zulfikar (CS) and Capt Izhar (5NLI) embraced shahadat and five other jawans also. I along with 10 jawans rushed to Badar to counter any possible enemy action. But enemy didn't dare. CO 5 NLI, doctor and Lt Khalid reached Badar soon by Hel and so I came back to Riaz after evac of cas.

June 17: Capt Asim and Maj Haq (5NLI) came to Riaz from Imtiaz. At night we slept in Shell bunker due to en arty shelling. At 0300 hrs, the wall of the bunker collapsed. I was sleeping beside the wall so stones fell on me but thanks Allah nothing serious happened except a few bruises.

June 18: 6th day in the sector. An Heli-borne operation is expected, so we are alert. During the day, we repaired the bunker.

June 19: We constructed another bunker but this time a larger one to accommodate a tent. Capt Sajid, ex 5 NLI joined today on his way down. At 2130 hrs, I received orders for tomorrow to move to Badar Base.

June 20: 8th day at Tanveer sub sector. I moved to Badar Base, reached there in two and a half hours. Nice speed. Maj Inam and Lt Khalid (5 NLI) were there. I got the orders to move to Hassan.

June 21: Spent the day at Badar and moved from Hassan at sunset. Reached Hassan in five hours – nice speed again. Capt Waheed (154 SP AD) and Capt Murtaza were there. I have to relieve Capt Murtaza (5 NLI).

June 25: 13th day in the sector. Kept constructing shell bunker the whole day. Enemy Mirage 2000 bombers kept reccying the area but didn't bomb. An SA-16 missile was fired on enemy aircraft but it escaped. Enemy shelling and rocketting kept on whole day. We are expecting 10-men party from

Badar base for ration and ammunition dump. A news – 8 NLI is relieved from Skardu. It is coming to Tanveer sector, will be here within a week.

June 26: Last night, party brought ration, K-II and my demand. I have got cigarettes, dry fruit, Everyday milk powder, so my adm is good now. It's a holy month and holy days. We pray a lot. Let Allah make it good for us.

June 27: 15th day in sector. Lot of shelling is going on. It's Eid Milad-ud-Nabi today.

June 30: Early morning, a shell landed in front of our tent. Tent was ripped apart by the splinters. Capt Waheed got a splinter injury in his left thigh. Although we were…

July 1: 19th day in sector. Lawar was attacked early morning but repulsed. At 1200 hrs, Aqil was reported to be attacked. CO 5 NLI told me to go and cut off enemy route. I reccied the area and told him the enemy is behind Aqil ridge and I can't leave my post vacant. So I didn't go…

Annexure B

Background on delineation of the Line of Control

Pervez Musharraf had been on Indian soil and the Indian Army believed all along that Pakistan would respect the delineation of the Line of Control. The fact that Musharraf had visited Skardu twice in early 1999 had also not been analysed by any of the agencies. As for our commanders, they seemed smug in the belief that the sanctity of the line of control would be maintained, at least in the Kargil sector.

The Simla Agreement signed by Zulfikar Ali Bhutto and Indira Gandhi stated: "In order to initiate the process of the establishment of durable peace, both the governments agree that: In Jammu and Kashmir, the line of control resulting from the ceasefire of December 17, 1971, shall be respected by both sides without prejudice to the recognized position of either side. Neither side shall seek to alter it unilaterally, irrespective of mutual differences and legal interpretations. Both sides undertake to refrain from threat or use of force in violation of this line."

A total of nine meetings preceded the document and were held between the senior commanders of the two countries between August 10, 1972 and December 11, 1972 alternatively at Suchetgarh near Jammu and Wagah near Amritsar. At each meeting, the inputs of subsectors were discussed, the sticky points resolved and where necessary, a joint survey was ordered to ensure that nothing was left vague or uncertain. Some issues were also amicably resolved by the army chiefs of both countries and for these, the meetings were held at Lahore in November and December between Field Marshal Sam Manekshaw and General Tikka Khan.

In this entire exercise, two sets of maps, each comprising 27 maps, were prepared. According to Lt Gen M.L. Chibber, who was the deputy director of Military Operations after the 1971 war, the marked maps were joined and 19 mosaics were prepared, thus clearly delineating the entire stretch of the LoC running through 740 km. Besides the maps, there were 19 annexures consisting of 40 pages, giving details of every feature, landmark and coordinate of the LoC. The delineated LoC was jointly prepared and signed by two senior military commanders, Lt Gen P.S. Bhagat and Lt Gen Hammed Khan. These documents were jointly signed and exchanged by the two senior military commanders on December 11, 1972 at Suchetgarh.

Immediately after the signing of the delineation maps and documents at the final meeting of senior military commanders on December 11, 1972, the DMO flew to New Delhi and reported to the chief of army staff (COAS) along with copies of the signed delineation proceedings and one copy of the signed maps at 1500 hours. The COAS presented these at a meeting of the Cabinet Committee on Political Affairs (CCPA) at 1600 hours the same day. At 1620 hours a message was received from Aziz Ahmed, special assistant to the president of Pakistan for P.N. Haksar, principal secretary to the prime minister, informing him that the Government of Pakistan had accorded its approval to the joint recommendations submitted by the senior military commanders of Pakistan and India on that day in regard to the delineation of the LoC in Jammu and Kashmir. This message was passed to the COAS at Parliament House and at 1747 hours, the DMO informed the DMO Pakistan Army on the telephone that the Government of India had accorded its approval to the joint recommendations.

At 0700 hours on December 17, 1972, the mutually agreed-upon statement was released in New Delhi and Islamabad. At 2100 hours on 20 December, a joint statement was released to the media regarding withdrawal of troops from the international border and delineation in conformity with the LoC in Jammu and Kashmir.

For 27 years, no one questioned the authenticity of the agreement until Pakistan Foreign Minister Sartaj Aziz made a statement that while the LoC was delineated on maps, it was not marked on the ground.

It was a blatant attempt to justify the intrusions and raise the Indo-Pakistan strategic stakes. Aziz, of course, forgot to mention Pakistan's training and military and logistical support to the armed insurgents which is in itself a violation of the Simla Agreement.

Glossary

1/3 GR	1/3 Gorkha Rifles
12 JAKLI	12 Jammu and Kashmir Light Infantry
2iC	Second in Command
AAR	After Action Report
ADS	Advance Dressing Station
AGLs	Automatic Grenade Launchers
Air Ops	Air Operations
ALG	Advance Landing Ground
APO	Army Post Office
arty	artillery
AWS	Advance Winter Stocking
Cas Evac	Casualty Evacuation
CGI	Corrugated Iron
CLGPs	Cannon Launched Guided Projectiles
COAS	Chief of Army Staff
CI Ops	Counter Insurgency Operations
CO	Commanding Officer
DGMO	Director General Military Operations
Div.	Division
DRDO	Defence Research & Development Organisation

ECC sleeping bags	Extremely cold climate sleeping bags
En	Enemy
FNCA	Force Commander Northern Area
FSC	Forward Surgical Centre
GOC	General Officer Commanding
HAPO	High Altitude Pulmonary Oedema
HAA	High Altitude Area
Heli Msn	Helicopter mission
hepter	helicopter
HUMINT	Human Intelligence
IB	Intelligence Bureau
JCO	Junior Commissioned Officer
LoC	Line of Control
MMGs	Medium Machine Guns
MI	Military Intelligence
Ni	Night
NLI	Northern Light Infantry
NVD	Night Vision Devices
RAPs	Regimental Medical Aid Post
RAW	Research and Analysis Wing
RPGs	Rocket Propelled Grenades
Raj. Rif.	Rajputana Rifles
recce	reconnaissance
RPVs	Remotely Piloted Vehicles
SAMs	Surface to Air Missiles
TCP	Traffic Check Post
WO	Warning Order

Index